# Marriage
# and
# Family Enrichment

THE *JOURNAL OF PSYCHOTHERAPY & THE FAMILY* SERIES:

# Marriage
# and
# Family Enrichment

Wallace Denton
Editor

The Haworth Press
New York • London

HQ
10
.M37325
1986
155 110
mar.1992

*Marriage and Family Enrichment* has also been published as *Journal of Psychotherapy & the Family,* Volume 2, Number 1, Spring 1986.

The Haworth Press, Inc., 28 East 22 Street, New York, NY 10010-6194
EUROSPAN/Haworth, 3 Henrietta Street, London WC2E 8LU England

**Library of Congress Cataloging-in-Publication Data**

Marriage and family enrichment.

   Published also as v. 2, no. 1 of the Journal of psychotherapy & the family.
   Includes bibliographies.
   1. Marriage counseling—Addresses, essays, lectures. 2. Group relations training—Addresses, essays, lectures. 3. Family—Addresses, essays, lectures. I. Denton, Wallace.
HQ10.M37325     1986     362.8′286          86-308
ISBN 0-86656-495-0

# Marriage and Family Enrichment

Journal of Psychotherapy & the Family
Volume 2, Number 1

## CONTENTS

## Marriage Enrichment: Rationale and Resources      111
### Sandra Diskin

# EDITORIAL NOTE

As our subscribers know, the purpose of the *Journal of Psychotherapy & the Family* is to present the most comprehensive and scholarly coverage of an issue vital to the general practitioner of psychotherapy. The *Journal* is very pleased to present this special issue that focuses on another critically important topic to the practice of psychotherapy: prevention.

Most observers would agree that professional clinical intervention with families has enjoyed steady growth for the last two decades. And within the last several years family-centered services have evolved from a few university centers and treatment programs, to its current popularity within nearly all social service sectors. More than ever before professionals are being trained to work with families and clients with family-related issues. The disciplines of psychotherapy too have embraced the family as a unit of analysis and intervention and implemented procedures and standards for family assessment and treatment. Yet the approach most frequently employed for systemic, emotional, or relationship problems is the same as the approach employed by most psychotherapists. Such an approach tends to promote amelioration or remediation, while ignoring the equally important goal of *prevention*.

The editor of this special issue is Wallace Denton. Dr. Denton is a long-time director of Purdue University's graduate training program in family therapy. It has an international reputation for one of the finest graduate training programs in family studies and therapy. In addition to being a popular professor, clinician, author and lecturer, he is a pioneer in mental health prevention in the area of marriage and the family. Years ago he developed what he called a ''preconflictual'' approach to marital counseling which emphasized prevention of major interpersonal problems. Similar to other early therapists, Denton emphasized relationship skill-building, empathic development between marriage partners, and a basic philosophy which emphasized the *strengths* of the marriage and family systems.

In this important collection, Denton dares to suggest in this era of emphasis on systemic psychopathology that psychotherapy must consider a significant paradigm shift. In contrast to viewing psychotherapy as a healing profession, Denton and his contributors emphasize the importance of enhancement and enrichment. It is an approach which, according to Denton " . . . calls for prevention, for helping couples and families to discover their strengths and enhance these before reaching the clinical stage" (p. 1).

The importance of prevention-oriented intervention programs and methods has recently been confirmed through a highly celebrated study summarized in a paper in this collection by Paul Giblin. Employing meta-analysis research methods which statistically aggregates and evaluates the empirical findings of 85 studies, Giblin concluded that clients clearly benefit from the prevention approach. Moreover, others throughout this collection suggest that enrichment programs, though not as dramatic as therapy, are frequently more effective in facilitating client change.

The *Journal* is dedicated to improving the art and science of psychotherapy practice by focusing on the role of the family. We see the role of the family as being among the most important social support system to the well-being of its members. When this system begins to experience major psychopathology, what transpires is in part chaos, relief, emotional pain, and a natural evolution of a dynamic system. This special issue, with its focus on prevention, provides us with an important alternative to psychotherapy. As efforts are made to make psychotherapy practice more effective in resolving relationship-centered emotional problems, enrichment programs and methods will become more common and accepted nationally. Wallace Denton and his contributors have provided an important benchmark for students, trainers and practitioners of psychotherapy to shape a more humane and proactive human service profession.

*Charles R. Figley, PhD*
*Editor*

# Introduction to
# Marriage and Family Enrichment:
# A Shift in the Paradigm

## Wallace Denton

Marriage and family enrichment represents a major shift in the paradigm of our approach to helping families. The traditional (or medical) model, exemplified in psychotherapy, calls for remediation, of repairing broken relationships. Of course, there is a place for this model. However, enrichment calls for prevention, for helping couples and families to discover their strengths and enhance these before reaching the clinical stage. Rather than waiting for something to "go wrong," enrichment is proactive. It takes the initiative to deal with the ordinary difficulties of life while they are just that—small, "stone-in-the-shoe" problems of living confronted by all couples and families. However, if unattended, if mismanaged, these everyday problems can blossom into crises of major proportions so that therapy *is* needed.

My first encounter with enrichment was serendipitous when I made an unscheduled visit to the Yokefellow Institute in Richmond, Indiana in the late 1960's. I found there a group of about twenty Methodist ministers and their wives who had spent the last day or so exploring their own marriage relationships. As they shared with me something of their experience, I was impressed not only with their contagious enthusiasm for what was happening, but also with the refreshing openness with which they shared with each other. So far as I know, no one had yet used the term "enrichment" to describe what was happening. I do remember thinking that this had exciting and powerful preventive possibilities. I later delivered a paper on the approach which I called "preconflictual marital counseling." Subsequently, I began experimenting with various approaches to working with couples in what we would now call enrichment.

The next significant occasion I remember was being one of the speakers at a national conference in Charlotte, North Carolina where David and Vera Mace, and Howard Clinebell, among others, were also

Wallace Denton, EdD, is Professor of Family Therapy in the Department of Child Development and Family Studies, Purdue University, West Lafayette, IN 47907.

on the program. David asked Howard and myself to have dinner with Vera and himself saying he had an idea he wanted to discuss. Over dinner, they said they had decided that marriage and family therapists were too busy with remediation to invest much energy in prevention. Yet, they were convinced that we must do something to prevent problems from arising. Furthermore, they thought there are vast untapped reservoirs of strength in the tens of thousands of couples across the nation who have strong marriages. However, they said, no vehicle has existed for bringing these couples together to pool their strengths and support each other. In the marriage enrichment movement they thought we at last had something which might bring these couples together. However, an organization was lacking to coordinate, promote, and bring into focus the potential in marriage enrichment. They were, therefore, thinking of founding a new group to be called by the acronym of ACME, standing for Association of Couples for Marriage Enrichment. ACME, they reminded us, is a GREEK word meaning the highest achievement. Their question to Howard and myself: What do you think of this idea? Two thoughts flooded my mind. The first was that I was flattered that David and Vera Mace, long heroes of mine, valued my input. The second thought was one in which both Howard and I concurred, that this was an outstanding idea, one whose time had come! We also agreed that it would require a massive effort to get the project launched. Illness, remediation, and repairing the broken has always somehow held more attraction than health, prevention, and enrichment. But, we were sure that if anyone could launch this project, David and Vera Mace were the ones who could do it. The next day they announced the idea of ACME to the conference.

In our throw away culture, we tend to discard broken and worn relationships onto the junk heap of broken dreams. Undaunted, partners start over again, often by going to that same junk heap to select a different (and formerly discarded) mate. True, sometimes that is about as good as can be done. However, the enrichment movement was born of optimism, an optimism that prevention (enrichment) can help keep many of those relationships from being thrown onto that junk heap.

This collection of essays is a major attempt to make a significant contribution to the enrichment movement. Written by some of the seminal thinkers in marriage and family enrichment, the collection also includes work by some of the bright, new, innovative, young scholars who are just now beginning to make their impact on the field. These new contributors build on the foundations already laid down by their forebearers in enrichment, but they also take it to new heights.

It is appropriate that the lead essay be by David and Vera Mace who write on "The History and Present Status of the Marriage and Family Enrichment Movement." In fact, any serious discussion of marriage and family enrichment would be incomplete without their input. They, more than anyone else in the United States, have been responsible for enrichment's growth and development. They were on the stage when the curtain first lifted on the drama of this movement. It is, therefore, appropriate that they review the history and present status of enrichment. They are the major writers of that history!

By its very nature, enrichment attracts those who are often primarily interested in the applied dimensions of the field. Therefore, five essays in this collection set forth specific enrichment programs. Each leader who decides to implement any one of these will obviously adapt each program to suit his or her own purposes and audience, but they will provide important beginning ideas and guidelines.

The first of these five approaches is one of the newer programs on enrichment scene, Training in Marriage Enrichment (TIME). In "Time for a Better Marriage," developers Don Dinkmeyer and Jon Carlson outline this ten session program. Each session covers issues of vital concern to couples as: communication, choice-making skills, conflict resolution, and goals setting. For those who are interested, cassettes and other helps are available which have been prepared by the developers.

The changing roles of women, their increasing education, and entry into increasingly significant positions of leadership has led to a new phenomenon which has been of growing interest in recent years—the dual career family. No enrichment program has been developed which specifically addresses itself to the needs of these families. Because of this, the contribution of Judith Myers Avis is important. Drawing on her expertise as a family therapist and enrichment leader, not to mention her own experience as a dual career family, she had developed a significant program for these couples.

Almost all enrichment programs are designed for couples. Little has been done for the family as a whole. For this reason, Margaret Sawin's contribution "Family Clusters Way to Family Enrichment" is especially important. One of the first enrichment programs to be developed, family clusters has been used mainly in church settings. Of course, this is because the church is among the few institutions to work with the entire family. However, this approach for bringing several families together doubtless has other applications in places where people have been brought together in our society. These include getting interested families together who live in the same apartment building, housing complex or other such setting. In any case, family clusters offers an approach for providing support for families who are scattered and separated from their roots by developing something of an "intentional family."

To date, marriage enrichment has been conducted in group settings. This raises the question as to whether any of the techniques used with groups can be adapted for an individual couple? Frederic Stevens and Luciano L'Abate answer this question in the affirmative. It is for this reason that their contribution "Structured Enrichment (SE) of a Couple" is important. Therapists will likely find this approach useful in those cases where the initial crisis is past and they are making significant progress in their relationship, yet termination is not yet in order. Such couples could very well benefit from Structured Enrichment.

Wallace Denton's contribution, "Developing a Local Marriage Enrichment Group," addresses itself to those who live in one of the countless communities across the nation where trained enrichment leadership is not readily available to lead a group. An approach is presented in which persons with relatively little training or background in enrichment can organize their own group. This is not to disparage programs led by trained leaders. Rather, it is a vehicle for bringing couples together for mutual support and give them a forum within which they can talk to each other as a couple when trained leaders are not available.

One thing which stands out in reading the enrichment literature is the repeated call by leaders in the field for more research. The research which Paul Giblin reports, "Research in Marriage and Family Enrichment: A Meta-Analysis Study," is a response to that need. It is perhaps the single most significant study done to date. Using a sophisticated research technique of meta-analysis, an analysis of 85 prior premarital, marital, and other enrichment studies were examined. As a result of his research, for the first time family specialists are able to say with some confidence that enrichment does indeed have the positive effect. Of course, much research remains to be done, but this is a significant major report.

In "Marriage Enrichment: Rationale and Resources," Sandra Diskin sets forth a rationale for marriage enrichment and then explores some of the resources available to those interested in enrichment. She provides names and addresses of a number of groups and agencies who offer enrichment services and publish materials for the enrichment leader. The reader will likely be surprised by how many different groups now offer enrichment, and this list is not exhaustive.

It is believed that this collection by some of the pioneers in the field of enrichment, as well as some of the bright, new faces, will provide one of the finest resources currently available for those interested in marriage and family enrichment.

# The History and Present Status of the Marriage and Family Enrichment Movement

David Mace
Vera Mace

**ABSTRACT.** The proposal is to provide family members with services on a *preventive* basis, proportionate to our present extensive *remedial* services. The enrichment concept aims at skills training which will develop inherent potential for creative relationships, instead of waiting until serious trouble develops and then trying to reverse the process. Modern expectations in marriage now focus on the quality of the *companionship* relationship, but fail to understand the complexities of the task. Appropriate training is the answer, and the behavioral sciences are now making this possible. The need is to provide such training on a wide scale.

What marriage and family enrichment represents is a shift in emphasis from remedial programs, designed to help families in trouble, to preventive programs, designed to keep families out of trouble, by enabling them to develop their own resources. Our purpose is not just to replace the remedial with the preventive, but rather to bring them both together. Our goal at this stage is to see every American community providing both preventive and remedial programs on a roughly equal basis—each involving about half of all the workers involved, and half of all the time and money spent. In this way the development of pathology will be attested at its source, and the focus of our efforts will be to foster what we like to call "family wellness." We prefer the term "wellness" to "health," because it is unambiguously positive. You can have either good health—or bad health; but you can't have bad wellness!

We believe it is now possible to develop programs to enable increasing numbers of people to enjoy the experience of family wellness. Families in trouble have now been extensively studied by the behavioral sciences. When a therapist sits down with a troubled family, one of the first things

David Mace, PhD, is Professor Emeritus of Family Sociology, Bowman Gray Medical School, Winston-Salem, NC. He and his wife, Vera Mace, MA, were for seven years (1960–67) Executive Directors of the American Association of Marriage Counselors (now the American Association for Marriage and Family Therapy). They are also founders (1973) of the Association of Couples for Marriage Enrichment (ACME).

7

he or she does is to take a case history, in order to diagnose the processes by which the trouble has developed up to its present critical point. Gathering such histories over and over again produces in time a clear and logical picture of the process of deterioration which precedes the crisis point. By putting all this knowledge together, it should surely be possible to identify the causes, and chart the progress of unhealthy interaction patterns which later drive the families concerned to seek the help of the therapist. With this knowledge, we should be able to devise creative services which enable more healthy interaction patterns to be established right from the beginning of family formation.

Notice that enrichment is not a process of "pumping in," from the outside, something that is not already there. It is rather a matter of drawing out inner resources that the family members already possess, but which they have been unable to use in order to achieve what they really want in their shared life.

This process offers no serious difficulties. It is a logical preventive action which is already in operation in many areas—like regular medical and dental check-ups, or taking regular exercise in order to keep fit. We could have developed preventive services to families already on an extensive scale if we had taken the necessary action. However, we have not taken action—virtually all our rapidly multiplying services to families are still remedial services. The reasons for this are quite clear, and we will discuss them later.

Meanwhile, let us look at the historical picture. We two are in a specially good position to do this, because we have been involved personally in the process from the very beginning.

In the year 1942, in the West End of London, we opened the first Marriage Guidance Center in England. There had been earlier attempts to provide marriage counseling in Europe—in Hitler's Germany, for example; but they had not survived. The London Center did survive. Indeed, it is still in operation today.

The opportunity to get this center started was provided by what happened in World War II. First, the men were called up for military service, and many of them sent overseas. Second, women took over the civilian services. Third, children were evacuated from the bombed cities. Family life was thus deeply fragmented, and help was desperately needed. In that situation, the Marriage Guidance Council, an organization which a small group of us had established in 1938, was ready with a plan. Over a period of seven years, we were able to develop a network of Marriage Guidance Centers all over Britain. In 1949 the British government was convinced of the importance of this project, and took over its operation. It has been supported by the government ever since.

Meanwhile, marriage counseling was also being developed in the United States. The idea originated here as early as the 1920's. (Ernest

Groves, for whom the Groves Conference is named, was one of the early pioneers.) In 1942 the American Association of Marriage Counselors was formed, but the organization was slow in developing. As late as 1960, it was in trouble, and had to close its only office, in New York City. At this point, we were invited to take it over. The view was that, since we had already developed a national service for marriage counseling in Britain, we might also be able to do the same here!

Reluctantly at first, we agreed to try. We became Executive Directors of the American Association of Marriage Counselors, and moved its headquarters office to the basement of our New Jersey home, where we spent another seven years developing the nucleus of a national organization. When we were sure it was a going concern, we handed it over to new leadership. It is today the American Association for Marriage and Family Therapy, with full professional recognition and over 12,000 clinical members.

Meanwhile, we had also been responding to requests from other countries for help in developing marriage counseling services. We spent six months developing a national service in South Africa, another four months in Australia, and a shorter period in New Zealand. All these are still functioning today. We also helped develop marriage counseling in a number of European countries.

After these efforts, we thought we had done whatever could be done to help marriages succeed. Alas, however, as we took time out to review our work, we saw only a steady increase in the number of troubled marriages. Had we failed? Was all the knowledge and skill we had developed an inadequate answer?

## THE NEED FOR PREVENTION

As we pondered this question, we gradually came to see the situation more clearly. We had begun with the idea that most marriages work out successfully, but that a few here and there get into trouble, and need help. During World War II years, trouble was of course, greatly multiplied; but we thought that in time things would return to normal. When this did not happen, we thought we just needed more counselors, and improved skills.

In time, however, we began to see a different picture. We realized that two big changes had occurred. First, the emancipation of women had changed marriage to a companionship relationship. This meant a two-vote system, which is much more difficult to manage than the one-vote system of the past. Also, we were moving to an acceptance of "no-fault divorce," making it very easy for people to walk out of a disappointing marriage. So while expectations of marriage were now much higher, we had done almost nothing to train couples in the new skills that had become necessary; and we had made it much easier to give up when the task became difficult.

Was there an answer? Yes, we thought there was. Our own marriage was working very well—and we knew a number of other couples who were very happy. What did they have that so many others were missing? We went back to something that had happened to us in 1962 while we were Executive Directors of the American Association of Marriage Counselors.

In October of that year, we had been asked to lead a weekend experience for a group of married couples at a retreat center in the mountains of Eastern Pennsylvania. These were not couples in trouble, but couples seeking to strengthen their marriage. We had never done anything like this before. However, it turned out to be a good experience, and we were asked to do another. Then there came more invitations— from New England, from Philadelphia, from the Midwest. We found ourselves enjoying these weekends, and learning a great deal.

For years we had been seeing the insides of marriages in serious trouble. Now we were seeing the insides of marriages where the couples were not seeking counseling, but only seeking to improve the quality of their relationships. We began to ask—"What is the difference between the two groups?"

It was not easy at first to answer that question. There were no dramatic differences. The only thing that was very clear was that the couples who came for counseling had almost no coping skills, while the other couples wanted to improve the skills they already had. Gradually it became clear to us that among all the resources that make a marriage successful, the possession of certain coping skills is the critical factor.

We realized that our counseling at that time was rather simplistic. We looked for "problems" and then developed standard solutions to apply to them. We now saw that "problems" were simply situations in the life of the couple, which we tried to patch up for them. We became more and more convinced that if we could only enable these couples to develop certain skills, they could solve (or prevent) their own problems. We saw that when marriages fail, they fail first on the *inside*. Then they become incapable of coping with *outside* situations. The art of marriage, it seemed to us, was to achieve a gradual adaptation to each other by a process of relational growth and behavioral change.

All this time we were continuing to lead weekend retreats for couples. As we developed better leadership skills, we were amazed at what could happen in so short a time as a weekend. We realized that most couples were secretly longing for a deeper and more satisfying relationship, but they did not know how to go about it; or if they did know, they were in a state of paralysis and could not get started. Somehow the retreat experience created the breakthrough which they needed.

By this time we believed we had found the answer for which we were searching. We saw that, while marriage counseling had to continue, we must also develop a parallel movement to get in at the preventive level. We had coined the term "marriage enrichment" to describe what was happening in our retreats. So now we made a big decision—to start a new organization. We called it the Association of Couples for Marriage Enrichment (ACME), and started it in 1973 on our 40th wedding anniversary.

## MARRIAGE ENRICHMENT GETS STARTED

While we had been pioneering this new approach, others had also been getting into the act.

The real beginning of marriage enrichment was in Barcelona, Spain, where Father Gabriel Calvo started the Catholic organization called Marriage Encounter. When we first met him, years later, and compared notes, we found that his first retreat had been in January 1962, whereas our had been in October of that same year. No earlier beginning that led to unbroken continuity has come to light.

After these beginnings, many people have developed experimental programs. Now the number has grown to the point at which involved couples run into the millions. We are not suggesting that all of these couples have experienced dramatic change. However, so many investigations have now been carried out, culminating in the recent major research of Giblin, Sprenkle, and Sheehan (1985), covering 3,886 couples and families in 85 enrichment events, that there can be no remaining doubt that enrichment produces positive results. Attempts to suggest that one form of marriage enrichment, Marriage Encounter, has negative results has failed to carry conviction (Doherty, McCabe, & Ryder, 1978). In fact, one of the wholly unexpected findings of the Giblin research is that couples who benefited most have been those who were in serious trouble—the very ones we have always discouraged, on the plea that what they needed was not enrichment, but therapy!

Although ACME and Marriage Encounter were first in the field, many other national and international groups have now developed. The great majority of them were first developed in religious settings. The churches are much more concerned about prevention of marriage breakdown than are the secular organizations. In addition, churches are the only community organizations that work extensively with entire families, so it was natural that they should seize eagerly something that looked like a promising answer. Almost all denominations now have some program of

marriage enrichment. The CAMEO organization (the Council of Affiliated Marriage Enrichment Organizations), which seeks to coordinate the
many national groups in the field, now has about 25 member organizations, which meet each year to report to each other and to share their
findings.

It should be made clear, however, that these various organizations
differ widely in the kinds of programs they offer. Some can hardly be
called marriage enrichment at all in any true sense. All of them are only
experimenting with something very new that has great promise, but
which as yet has scarcely begun to explore its full possibilities. Marriage
enrichment is going to be with us for a long time, and will become the
object of extensive study and research.

Something should now be said about these wider implications. While
the enrichment concept began with a sharp focus on the marital dyad, it
has now been more widely extended. It was soon found that when the
married couple learned to develop new skills in the management of their
own relationship, this often led to changes in their interactions with their
children, with other relatives, and with people in general. Now the door
was opened to parent enrichment, and we have often been impressed by
the way in which the children have adopted the new patterns of behavior
which their parents had discovered. This in turn has led to programs of
whole family enrichment, of which the main pioneer has been Margaret
Sawin (1979), and her Family Cluster Programs.

## BASIC THEORETICAL CONCEPTS

We now need to focus attention on the process of enrichment and the
theoretical frame of reference in which it has been developed.

There was a time when marriage counseling was described as ''a
practice in search of a theory'' (Manus, 1966). We never felt that this
represented a fair judgment. Even more so, we hope it is not true of
marriage enrichment; because from the beginning, as far as we are
concerned, it began with a theory about helping marriages, which we then
proceeded to test out in practice. The basic outline of that theory has
already been briefly described. Now we must go into more detail.

Although it appears that marriage has always existed in human culture,
in one form or another, its focus has been in two basic directions—first,
to produce children and to train them to continue the cultural values; and
second, to give continuity to family tradition and property. The actual
relationship between the marriage partners has never been given much
attention, and the concept of love and companionship between man and
woman has hardly ever been associated with the marriage relationship.
Marriages have been arranged as a matter of convenience, regardless of

how the persons involved felt about each other. William Walsh, an English poet, wrote in the 17th century that he loved his lady friend too much to want to marry her. "She is my queen," he said, "and I don't want to make her my slave." Today, however, the earlier purposes of marriage have receded into the background, and the ideal of a close relationship has become the primary goal. There is nothing wrong with that, except that apart from sexual attraction, we know almost nothing about how to establish a close relationship between a man and a woman. We have tried to fill the gap by suggesting that the more alike the two are, the better they will "fit" each other—we call it "compatibility." It really goes back to Plato's idea that people first existed as man-woman pairs joined together; but that the gods, in a mischievous mood, tore them apart, and now each of us must hunt around for his or her lost other half, then we will be united in a perfect fit.

This has produced the fatalistic idea that people "get married" on their wedding day; and if they "fit," all will be well. If not, they must just accept the situation "for better or for worse"; or, as so often happens today, divorce and hope for a better "fit" the second time around.

There's nothing wrong with looking for as much compatibility as possible at the start. But the idea that any couple would always be alike, and want to do the same thing in the same way at the same time, is absurd. What we say in marriage enrichment is that compatibility is the *goal* of marriage, and not the starting point. It is much less a state of affairs than a job of work; and whether the marriage turns out "for better or for worse" depends almost entirely on how the couple make use of the raw materials they bring to each other. In other words, marriage is an ongoing task achieved by a mutual process of joint personality growth and behavior change, in which differences are as important as similarities, and possession of the appropriate skills to interact creatively is the decisive factor. Building a marriage is, therefore, a task very similar to building a house or cultivating a garden.

It follows, then, that our new expectation of marriage as a deeply satisfying interpersonal relationship, combined with our almost total failure to train couples in the use of the necessary skills to achieve this goal, is all the explanation we need for the devastating breakdown of family life which we witness today. Marriage and family enrichment is simply a movement toward correcting this grave omission in our public policy. What we are doing, crudely at present, is trying to provide couples with the basic skills which they should have been given at the time when they embarked on the marriage relationship. The implication is that the ideal way to provide marriage enrichment is to guide couples through their first year together, which is what we believe in ACME.

## SKILLS NEEDED FOR SUCCESS IN MARRIAGE

Let us now focus on the skills necessary for a happy marriage. What we set out to do was to identify the "coping system" that was almost wholly lacking in the couples who got into serious trouble, but was greatly desired by the couples who came to our retreats. We checked this out all the time in our own relationship, in which, as a result of our efforts in marriage enrichment, we have seen very gratifying progress.

We are still trying to clarify our theoretical frame of reference; but so far we have broken down the "coping system" into what we call the "three essentials." Given all three, we think a couple have almost a guarantee of success. Without any of them, or all of them, almost inevitably a couple will fall short of what we call their "relational potential."

The first essential is a *commitment*, on the part of both partners, to work together for the building of a relationship that will meet, as far as possible, the needs of both; and to make all possible behavior changes that will further that end. They will thus have what we call an "intentional" marriage—they will have put together a "growth plan" toward which they are working, with clearly defined goals. Every couple involved in a retreat led by us will register privately, in writing and jointly signed, a growth plan, with built-in contracts for the following 12 month period. We find that, without this kind of specific action, they tend not to follow through. In local ACME chapters, member couples are encouraged to join "support groups" in which they may enlist the continuing help of other couples in fulfilling their goals over time.

The second essential is *an effective communication system*. It is now clearly understood that an intimate relationship simply cannot be sustained without a continuing state of openness and honesty. As misunderstandings and evasions multiply and pile up, there is a progressive drifting apart which leads to increasing alienation. Much has been learned in recent years about couple communication, and we have gratefully used these new insights in our programs. We ourselves, and many other couples, have found that the best way to sustain communication is to commit ourselves to a daily sharing time in which inner thoughts and feelings are clarified together, so that each knows just where the other is.

The third essential is the one which is least understood and yet, for many couples, the most important. It is *to make creative use of all conflicts that develop in the relationship*. Our culture often sees marital conflict as something evil, something to be avoided if at all possible in order to keep the peace. On the contrary, we now see conflict as the inevitable consequence of the differences between us, which become disagreements because in our quest for intimacy we have chosen to reduce our individual living space. The process follows three stages—

first, difference plus closeness becomes disagreement. Second, disagreement about action challenges individual freedom to act. Third, violation of individual freedom generates anger, which we define as the defense system of the ego. This process is elaborated in the book *Love and Anger in Marriage* by David Mace (1982).

These critical experiences are, therefore, vital and inevitable signals which point us to areas where, if we are to grow in closeness, we must work through our differences. We think "marital fighting" is a crude and ineffectual way of dealing with marital conflict, though it may be better than suppression and avoidance of the issue. We see both love and anger in marriage as healthy and positive emotions, which should be used together to bring about a balanced relationship which fosters intimacy without violation of individual personhood.

Our goal in marriage enrichment, therefore, is to encourage couples to learn and use these vital and essential resources; and if they are ready to do so, we have every reason to believe that they will avoid the kinds of interpersonal troubles that are breaking up marriages today on a disturbing scale.

We take the view, however, that some couples are unable to learn and use these essential skills, because of personality disorders that can best be cleared up by therapy. We shall always need therapists to deal with these situations. And there are couples who lack the ability, or the motivation, to make the behavior changes which marriage enrichment requires.

How, in practice, do we go about training couples to develop these skills? Could this be done in a teaching program, as in family life education?

With great reluctance we have to acknowledge that we do not find the classroom pattern of education effective in translating the necessary information into applied action. Before information can lead to behavioral change, it must pass through a long series of complex processes—stored knowledge, personal insight, experimental action, attitudinal change, and finally behavioral change sustained over time. Each stage *must involve the two persons acting together.* The entire process, as we see it, normally takes at least a year, with both partners participating together at each point, and in most cases within an effective support system. Behavioral change is not easy to bring about, and should not be. But the tragedy is that within our culture, and especially in marriage, we have often adopted the view that such change is not even *possible.* It may not be possible to change your *personality.* But your behavior is the way you choose to *use* your personality to gain what you want—and that is always possible. James Peterson, who headed up the major research (the Ethel Percy Andrus Center program) carried out by the American Association of Retired Persons at the University of Southern California, expressed it to us in these words—"We have now learned that old people can change their behavior up to the day of their death."

## THE NEED FOR FURTHER PROGRESS

We have probably said enough to give you a fairly clear picture of the marriage enrichment movement. Its effectiveness has now been demonstrated (Giblin, Sprenkle, & Sheehan, 1985), and its possibilities are exciting. Why, then, is it not getting widespread public support? To answer that question we must go back and describe briefly the two reasons referred to earlier.

The first is what we call the "intermarital taboo" (Mace, 1976). There exists in our culture an unwritten rule that married couples must never communicate to others what is going on in their interpersonal relationship. We often say that it would be fairly easy to get members of a church to kneel down together and repeat—"We are miserable sinners, and in need of repentance." But it would be an altogether different matter to ask a group of couples in that same church to stand together and say, "Our marriages are mediocre, and in need of enrichment."

Married couples who meet socially seldom refer to any difficulties they may be experiencing in their relationship, or ask each other for help. Since they are married, they are expected to be "living happily ever after", it would be embarrassing and humiliating for them to tell their friends that all is not well, and that as a couple they need help.

This is slowly changing; but we still have a long way to go before couples can be open and honest about their needs. Consequently, those who are in trouble tend to wait until the situation is desperate before they take any action; by which time it may be too late.

The second reason why the movement has not been enthusiastically embraced by the public is linked to the first. Because couples are embarrassed about seeking help until they are in really bad trouble, therapists cannot get them to come earlier, when more could be done for them because their motivation would be stronger.

A third reason may also be added. When people are really hurting they become desperate and are willing to pay for help. So to some extent, marriage counseling then becomes locked into what we call the "pain-gain formula"—"When your pain is severe enough, you will be willing to pay me enough for my services to enable me to earn a decent living." Many therapists would much prefer to do preventive work with couples; but they often say, "I can't afford to work on that basis—there's no money in it." This is entirely reasonable. Professionally trained people must be rewarded financially in order to go on functioning.

These situations could change, and we think they will change in time.

At present they are together causing the enrichment approach to make very slow progress. Our hope is that the time will come when young couples, or their parents, will be prepared to pay an adequate fee to have the couple guided through their first critical year together by a competent professional. Some small beginnings have been made in this direction, with very encouraging results.

Let us in conclusion put the issue in a wider context. The behavioral sciences consist mainly of people who belong to two disciplines— psychology, which puts its focus on the individual; and sociology, which puts its focus on the group. Along the boundary, not clearly claimed by either, is the dyad—two people interacting with each other. In earlier years, there was a tendency for neither discipline to focus on the issue of close dyadic relationships, but for each to leave it to the other.

That era is now past. We are seeing more and more clearly that the understanding of dyadic interaction is the key to human behavior as a whole. Our exploration of close relationships is moving ahead quickly. Marriage is by no means the only form of dyadic interaction; but it occupies a very basic place. Its effectiveness becomes the model for all who try marriage, which means very nearly everyone. It is, also, the dyadic model which is presented to the great majority of children, who are our future citizens. If dyadic interaction on a wide scale could be made to function really creatively, that could profoundly change the whole of human society for the better. We might truly say that this could be the most vital key to world peace, which is in turn the most vital key to our human future.

We are well aware that marriage enrichment seems, at the moment, to be a trivial and unimportant side issue in a busy world involved in a multitude of seemingly much more important matters. But those of us who are involved in it do not see it in that narrow perspective. We see it as the possible foundation stone of our viable human future.

## REFERENCES

Doherty, W.J., McCabe, P. & Ryder, R.G. (1978). Marriage encounter: A critical appraisal. *Journal of Marriage & Family Counseling, 4*(4), 99–107.

Giblin, P., Sprenkle, D. & Sheehan, R. (1985). Enrichment outcome research: A meta-analysis of premarital, marital and family findings. *Journal of Marital and Family Therapy, 11*(3).

Mace, D. (1982). *Love and Anger in Marriage.* Grand Rapids, MI: Zondervan.

Mace, D. & Mace, V. (1976). Marriage enrichment: A preventive group approach for couples. In David H.L. Olson (Ed.), *Treating Relationships* (pp. 321–336). Lake Mills, IA: Graphic Publishing.

Manus, G.I. (1966). Marriage counseling: A technique in search of a theory. *Journal of Marriage and the Family, 28*, 449–453.

Sawin, M.M. (1979). *Family Enrichment with Family Clusters.* Valley Forge, PA: Judson Press.

# BOOKS BY THE MACES ON MARRIAGE
# AND FAMILY ENRICHMENT

We Can Have Better Marriages—If We Really Want Them. Nashville, TN: Abingdon, 1974.
*Marriage Enrichment in the Church*. Nashville, TN: Broadman, 1976.
*How to Have a Happy Marriage*. Nashville, TN: Abingdon, 1979.
*Love and Anger in Marriage*. Grand Rapids, MI: Zondervan, 1982.
*Close Companions—The Marriage Enrichment Handbook*. NY: Continium, 1982.
*Prevention in Family Services—Approaches to Family Wellness*. Beverly Hills, CA: Sage, 1983.

# TIME for a Better Marriage

Don Dinkmeyer
Jon Carlson

**ABSTRACT.** This article presents a rationale and theory for the Training in Marriage Enrichment (TIME) program. A detailed description of this systematic approach to marital enrichment is provided. The skills of effective marriage are discussed.

The movement to enrich marriages and to provide education rather than therapy for couples began only two decades ago. This movement emerged to help couples build happier and more satisfying relationships. The historical routes of marriage enrichment are generally traced to Barcelona, Spain, where a group of married couples met in January, 1962, for a weekend marriage enrichment retreat with Father Gabriel Calbo. It is from this meeting that the world-wide network of marriage encounter resulted.

In October, 1962, David and Vera Mace, at that time executive directors of American Association of Marriage Counselors (now American Association for Marriage and Family Therapy) began leading weekend enrichment sessions for married couples in the United States. In 1973, the Maces founded the Association of Couples for Marriage Enrichment (ACME), an organization whose slogan is "To work for better marriages, beginning with our own".

In 1975, various enrichment organizations met together in Chicago to form a coordinating group now known as the Council of Affiliated Marriage Enrichment Organizations, or CAMEO. Rather than centering on the problems couples experience, these organizations focus on the need to teach couples the skills to build loving, intimate relationships. Marriage enrichment organizations have grown significantly in the last two decades, benefiting thousands of couples and laying the groundwork for new understanding of the marriage relationship. With this wider awareness of the concept of marriage enrichment and its benefits, there is now a growing demand for programs. Churches, in particular, are be-

Don Dinkmeyer, PhD, is President of the Communication and Motivation Training Institute, 4010 NW 99th St., Coral Springs, FL 33065.

Jon Carlson, EdD, is a psychologist and Director of the Lake Geneva Wellness Clinic, 101 Broad St., Suite 204, Lake Geneva, WI 53147.

coming more involved in providing marriage growth experiences for their members. Community service organizations are beginning to offer programs in marriage enrichment. Educational institutions increasingly understand their responsibility in providing course offerings.

In response to the needs for a skill-based marriage program that would allow couples to build a loving, satisfying, lasting relationship, Training in Marriage Enrichment (TIME) was developed.[1]

## INTRODUCTION

TIME is an educational program designed to help married couples learn the skills they need to build a loving, supportive relationship. In TIME groups, couples develop skills that enable them to enrich their marriage and to deal with particular challenges that they experience. Couples define the marriage they want and develop and retain the skills to maintain that relationship. Participation in a TIME group does not imply that a couple has an ineffective marriage or marriage problems. Rather, a couple's participation is an indication that they want to *grow* and want to *strengthen* their relationship.

TIME can be used in a wide variety of settings including:

1. A ten-session weekly marriage enrichment program
2. An intensive weekend workshop or retreat
3. A beginning experience for an ongoing marriage support group
4. Church study group, adult education program or university course in family life, counselor training or home economics
5. Support material for marriage and family therapists
6. Individual sessions related to individual TIME skills can be offered
7. A followup experience for couples who have been in marriage encounter or marriage enrichment groups

## THE TIME THEORY

TIME primarily reflects an Adlerian (Adler, 1931; Dreikurs, 1950) or sociopsychological approach to human relations. Many concepts are similar to those appearing in Systematic Training for Effective Parenting (STEP) Dinkmeyer and McKay, 1976 and Systematic Training for Effective Parenting of Teens (STEP/Teen) (Dinkmeyer and McKay, 1983).

The basic assumption underlying Adlerian theory is that "people are indivisible, social, decision making beings whose actions and psychological movement have a purpose'' (Dinkmeyer, Pew, and Dinkmeyer, 1979). We behave according to the expectations of the social group where we seek to belong. We seek to understand marital relationships in terms of their purpose. The goal is the final reason for behavior. We do not seek a causal explanation. There is no blaming of the past, parents, or other external factors. Instead, we look for the purpose of the symptom which keeps the marriage from being enriched. We believe marriages can be enriched because each partner has the capacity to choose, to act, not react. Man is relatively self-determining.

We behave according to how things seem to us, and the subjective perceptions we create. Our behavior thus is always a function of perceptions. However, perceptions can be modified through educational and enriching experiences.

An enriched marriage can be contrasted with the marriage which experiences infrequent enthusiasm, energy, commitment, and mutual involvement. In an enriched marriage, each spouse has a feeling of personal worth and self esteem. Each is willing to cooperate in the give and take of the relationship, to be willing at times to give without expecting to immediately receive. The system, then, is open, congruent, and cooperative.

## LEADERSHIP ROLE IN TIME

The leadership role focuses on promoting involvement and dialogue. The leader serves as a facilitator whose goal is to stimulate questions and encourage involvement in the exercises. The leader need not be an expert on marriage enrichment. Actually, too much expertise which encourages the leader to launch into lectures is a deterrent to the couple and the group process.

The leader's role is to create an atmosphere and a process which promotes growth between participating spouses. The leader makes materials available, presents the program for each session, leads discussions and exercises, guides the group to stay within the structure of the program, helps members apply the ideas, and encourages members to do the exercise assignments.

It is recommended that leaders be married couples. Effective leaders become a model for the group in relating, communicating, and resolving issues. They believe that encouragement is a major force for bringing about positive change. They regularly use encouragement skills in the group process and specific couples.

Encouragement is basic to the TIME enrichment process. Encouragement provides the unconditional acceptance and valuing that all married partners need, regardless of whether their marriages currently are satisfying or unsatisfying.

While encouragement is a philosophy and attitude, it must be implemented by specific actions and skills.

Some specific ways to put encouragement into practice:

1. The leader can begin sessions by asking, "What's new and positive in your marriage?" This helps couples to refocus on the progress they are making.
2. Share with members your positive feelings and observations: "I like the way you listen," "That sounds encouraging."
3. Encourage any movement towards incorporating "Encouragement Meetings" and "Encouraging Days" into their lives. Encouragement Meetings provide a regular, systematic way to allow each partner to share the positive things they are seeing in each other and the relationship. Encouraging Days is a vehicle for learning what pleases your partner and ways to provide it on a daily basis.
4. Have an Encouragement Meeting in a session, asking members to share what they like about the way the marriage enrichment experience is going for them.
5. Encourage members to share any positive experience. They can begin with phrases such as, "I enjoyed . . . ", "I like . . ." or "I appreciated."
6. Have members write down 5 personal strengths that enable them to be encouraging partners.

## *BASIC PRINCIPLES OF TIME*

TIME is based upon the following principles:

1. Developing and maintaining a good marriage relationship requires a time commitment. For a marriage to succeed, couples must make their relationship an important priority now and in the future.
2. Specific skills essential to a healthy marriage can be learned. When partners understand how a marriage works and the necessary skills for building a successful marriage, they can develop skills that create a positive, rewarding relationship.
3. Change often takes time, but all change begins with the individual. The first step in enriching a marriage involves a commitment to change. Partners begin by understanding how they each have shaped their marriage and what each can do to make desired changes. Change takes time. Couples are encouraged to be patient with their rates of progress.

4. Feelings of love and caring that have diminished or disappeared often return with behavior changes. Romantic feelings, intimacy and love may diminish over time in a marriage relationship. When feelings change, many couples needlessly believe that the relationship is over. The change in feelings may mean that partners are not being reinforced in the marriage and that the relationship deserves a higher priority. By viewing their relationship as intimate and satisfying, a couple can establish new behavior and feelings.

5. Small changes are very important in bringing about big changes. A happier relationship results from many small changes over a period of time. Even though both partners are committed to change, there may be times when unwanted patterns reappear. This does not mean that their new skills are not working. Couples are encouraged to continue focusing on the positive relationship they want.

## MARRIAGE SKILLS

The TIME Program is organized systematically. Each of ten sessions is designed to present basic principles and provide opportunities to practice the necessary skills for enriching a marriage. The goal is to help couples apply and integrate the ideas and skills into their marriage relationship. This goal is achieved through reading, meaningful discussions and application of the ideas and activity assignments and exercises. The couple is expected to work on specific skills, i.e. Daily Dialogue, Encouragement Meetings to assess goals and progress through the My Plan format. A cassette, *Time to Relax and Imagine*, is a personal audiocassette designed to improve the marital relationship.[2]

In TIME sessions, couples learn and apply the following skills: to accept responsibility for their behavior, to identify and align goals, to encourage each other, to identify factors that influence a marriage relationship and understand their responsibility in creating the desired relationship, to communicate honestly and congruently, to make choices that support marriage goals (e.g., choices of thoughts, words and actions), learn a process for resolving conflict, apply the conflict resolution to common marital challenges such as children, money, in-laws, friends, sex, religion, recreation, alcohol and drug abuse; and they commit to the process of maintaining an equal marriage.

## PROGRAM

Participants prepare for each session by reading in advance the appropriate chapter of the couple resource book, *TIME for a Better Marriage* (Dinkmeyer and Carlson, 1984).

The sequence of the session is as follows:

1. Building Communication. Several activities are used that focus on building communication. The activities are usually done as couples, but may involve some group interaction. These activities are designed to create an atmosphere of readiness for ensuing activities.
2. Discussion of Activity for the Week. Each week couples are expected to do one or more activities that reinforce the skill introduced in the previous session. At this point in the session, couples share their experience working with the activities of the week, followed by group discussion to provide support and encouragement. It is essential that couples participate regularly and enthusiastically in the activity assignments. These activities help to improve the marital relationship.
3. Discussion of Reading. Participants express their ideas, feelings and attitudes which emerge as a result of the reading assignment. The discussion focuses on what they learned about themselves and their relationship.
4. Presentation of the Recording. The audio tapes for each session focus on the skill presented in the session. Participants practice the skill by responding to the audio-recorded interactions.
5. Application. The skill or concept introduced in the session is experienced and practiced through an activity.
6. My Plan is found at the end of each chapter and is a form on which partners write their concerns and commitments and assess their progress each week.
7. Summary. The summary is an essential part of each session. Each member contributes and identifies what he or she has learned during the session.
8. Activities and Reading for the Week. This is the assignment of the week's activity and reading for the session.

### Session 1: Accepting Responsibility

Session 1 focuses on the need for partners to individually accept responsibility for their behavior and for the success of their marriage. Couples learn about the positive goals of marriage—cooperation, contributing, accepting responsibilities, and encouraging, and they learn to recognize relationship-destroying goals—excusing shortcomings, power, control and vengeance. They learn the importance of spending planned time together and preserving time for relaxation and time alone through a process called Daily Dialogue. They establish a daily time for sharing.

## Session 2: Encouragement

Session 2 introduces the skills of encouragement which include unconditional acceptance, recognizing effort, focusing on strengths, listening, empathy, being enthusiastic, creating positive meanings or perceptual alternatives. It helps couples establish encouragement meetings and encouraging days; important activities that bring encouragement to their marriage on a regular basis. The importance of self-encouragement is also discussed.

## Session 3: Priorities and Values

In Session 3, couples develop a better understanding of factors that influence their relationships including their priorities, lifestyle, values and destructive "games." They learn to identify their priorities and values. Discussions of life style priorities include Control, Superiority, Pleasing, and Comfort Seeking. The games that couples play are sophisticated, patterned maneuvers that are destructive to a marriage relationship. They tend to focus on individual power rather than on the growth of the relationship. Couples are taught to develop game-free relationships characterized by flexibility and empathy.

## Session 4: Congruent Communication

Session 4 introduces the concept of congruent communication which involves expressing whatever we are feeling and experiencing at the moment. Partners identify their communication style. Four negative styles are: The Placator, the Blamer, the Super Reasonable Communicator, and The Irrelevant Communicator (Satir, 1972). Couples develop skills by using "I messages" which indicate that they are sharing a subjective view. Partners learn to express feelings and thoughts openly without being insensitive to their partner's needs.

## Session 5: Listening and Responding to Whole Messages

In Session 5, couples develop understanding of how beliefs, feelings and goals influence communication. Partners practice communicating their thoughts and feelings on subjects of concern in their relationship. The following guidelines are recommended for improving communication:

1. Be aware of the feelings being shared.
2. Be aware of the intentions being shared.
3. Be aware of the beliefs being shared.

4. Strive for level, equal communication.
5. Be empathic. Hear, identify, and verbalize the other person's feelings.
6. Be responsible for your feelings.
7. Free each other to be. Encourage uniqueness.

### Session 6: Communication Skills

Session 6 provides couples the opportunity to practice effective listening skills, to hear the full message in the partner's words and to indicate that they have heard and understood feelings as well as thoughts. This involves understanding nonverbal behavior and developing an awareness of our ideas, intentions, and feelings in order to communicate honestly, fully, and accurately. Also, guidelines for the marriage meeting are introduced and couples learn the procedure for marriage meetings.

### Session 7: Choice-Making Skills

Session 7 focuses on the process of making choices that are helpful to a relationship and provides practice in identifying available choices and applying choicemaking skills. When couples delay making choices that can improve marriage, they are in effect choosing to keep the marriage as it is. The importance of being realistic and honest with oneself and the partner when making choices is emphasized. They are encouraged to make choices they can or will act upon. Choices are helpful when they encourage the development of a better relationship and harmful when they restrict the marriage.

### Session 8: Conflict Resolution Process

Session 8 introduces the four step conflict resolution process: show mutual respect, pinpoint the real issue, identify areas of agreement, and mutually participate in decisions. To resolve conflict, be specific and concentrate on the present and future rather than past. Couples establish a procedure for using the four step process. They also develop skills in dealing with anger.

### Session 9: Applying the Conflict Resolution Process

Session 9 continues the development of conflict resolution skills. Couples apply the four step process to an issue of concern in their relationship. The following areas of concern are highlighted: sex, finances, recreation, children, in-laws, religion, friends, and alcohol and drugs.

## Session 10: Equal Marriage

Session 10 enables couples to clarify what they have learned in the TIME Program and to identify and discuss marriage goals for the next 6 months. The following self-help procedures for maintaining an equal marriage are offered:

a. Encourage each other often.
b. Communicate frequently.
c. Deal with conflict.
d. Develop the courage to be imperfect.
e. Support each other fully.
f. Spend regular time together having fun.
g. Be aware of choices you can make in your relationship.
h. Develop shared dreams, goals, and interests.
i. Be self-accepting.
j. Have realistic expectations.

The time for counselors, therapists, and clergy to consider the value of marriage enrichment has arrived. This article provides a theory and process for working effectively with couples on the enrichment process.

## FOOTNOTES

1. TIME leaders include leaders from all of the helping professions: psychologists, psychiatrists, social workers, counselors, clergy and others. Leadership training with TIME materials and concepts is available through the publisher, American Guidance Service, or CMTI, Box 8268, Coral Springs, FL 33065.
2. TIME materials are available from American Guidance Service, Circle Pines, MN 55014, or 1-800-328-2560.

## REFERENCES

Adler, Alfred (1931). *What Life Should Mean to You*. New York: Capricorn Books.
Carlson, Jon (1978). *The Basics of Discipline*, Coral Springs, FL: CMTI Press.
Dinkmeyer, Don and Carlson (1984). *Time for a Better Marriage*. New York: Random House.
Dinkmeyer, Don and McKay, Gary (1976). *Systematic Training for Effective Parenting (STEP)* Circle Pines, MN: American Guidance Service. *STEP Handbook*, Dinkmeyer, Don and McKay, Gary D. (1982). New York: Random House.
Dinkmeyer, Don and McKay, Gary D. (1983). *Systematic Training for Effective Parenting of Teens (STEP/Teen)*. Circle Pines, MN: American Guidance Service.
Dinkmeyer, Don and Losoncy, Lew (1980). *The Encouragement Book*. Englewood Cliffs, NJ: Prentice-Hall.
Dinkmeyer, Don; Pew, W. L. and Kindmeyer, Don Jr. (1979). *Adlerian Counseling and Psychotherapy*. Monterey, CA: Brooks/Cole.
Dinkmeyer, Don. (1977). *The Basics of Self Acceptance*. Coral Springs, FL: CMTI press.

Dinkmeyer, Don (1976). *The Basics of Adult-Teen Relationships.* Coral Springs, FL: CMTI Press.
Dinkmeyer, Don Jr. and Dinkmeyer, Jim (1980). *The Basics of Parenting.* Coral Springs, FL: CMTI Press.
Dreikurs, R. (1950). *Fundamentals of Adlerian Psychology.* Chicago: Greenburg.
McKay, Gary D. (1976). *The Basics of Encouragement.* Coral Springs, FL, CMTI Press.
Satir, Virginia (1972). *Peoplemaking.* Palo Alto, CA: Science and Behavior Books.

# "Working Together":
# An Enrichment Program
# for Dual-Career Couples

## Judith Myers Avis

**ABSTRACT.** This article presents an enrichment program designed to respond to the particular needs and stresses of dual-career couples: renegotiating roles and responsibilities; structuring and managing time; meeting emotional needs; dealing with competition; and sharing control and power. The program consists of seven two-and-a-half hour weekly sessions. Designs for the sessions are described in detail to facilitate their use.

Dual-career couples represent a small but rapidly growing subgroup among today's married population. Over the past two decades, increasing numbers of women have entered careers before marriage, or returned to school and entered careers either during or after childbearing. Goldenberg and Goldenberg (1984) predicted that "by 1985, considering swollen university enrollments in which women pursue career-oriented goals, greater career opportunities for women, two-career couples living together outside of marriage, as well as greater social acceptance of the two-career phenomenon, we will be dealing with approximately five million dual-career families" (p. 30). These are the couples who are attempting to balance marriage, an active family life, and two professional careers.

The enrichment program presented here is designed specifically to respond to the needs of such couples, "where both individuals either already hold or are preparing educationally for positions in the professional, technical or managerial areas of the occupational structure" (Rice, 1979, p. 3). Such careers characteristically develop continuously over time and demand an intensity of involvement, a commitment of time and energy, and a level of training (both initial and ongoing) which are qualitatively different from those required by other occupations

Judith Myers Avis, MSW, is an assistant professor, Department of Social Work, St. Thomas University, Fredericton, New Brunswick, Canada E3B 5G3 (on leave), and a doctoral candidate in the Family Therapy Program, Department of Child Development and Family Studies, Purdue University, W. Lafayette, IN 47907.

*29*

(Rapoport & Rapoport, 1976). They consequently offer serious competition to the time and energy required by marriage and family life and often are accompanied by ''marital conflict, fatigue, a drain of limited energy, guilt feelings, in women, over not fulfilling customary role expectations at home, and discomfort, in men, over assuming new and unaccustomed roles in addition to their historical ones'' (Goldenberg & Goldenberg, 1984, p. 31). Careers also tend to offer greater personal satisfaction, financial benefits, life options and social status, resulting in a unique blend of joys and stresses for those pursuing this lifestyle. Although still sparse, a beginning literature examines this lifestyle and the particular problems encountered by dual-career couples as they work out a structure which fits their lives (Bird, 1979; Goldenberg & Goldenberg, 1984; Hall & Hall, 1979; Kimball, 1983; Pepitone-Rockwell, 1980; Rapoport & Rapoport, 1969, 1976; Rice, 1979; Shaevitz & Shaevitz, 1980; Stapleton & Bright, 1976). The most common issues and problems will be briefly summarized below to provide a context for this enrichment program and a rationale for its design.

## SOURCES OF STRESS IN DUAL-CAREER MARRIAGES

### Conflict Over Roles and Responsibilities

Although there are many benefits to both men and women in dual-career marriages, such as shared responsibility for economic support of the family, greater wife satisfaction, and greater access for both spouses to opportunities for continued growth and development, there are also definite stresses. Conflict over roles and responsibilities, particularly parenting and homemaking, is a frequent source of stress. Traditional gender-role socialization predisposes both men and women to regard these areas as primarily the wife's responsibility, even when she is pursuing a full-time career. As a result, most career women retain major responsibility for children, and even the most highly trained professional women tend to do their own housework without assistance from their husbands and without paid household help (Bird, 1979; Johnson & Johnson, 1977; Scanzoni, 1978; Tavris & Wade, 1984). Consequently, these women work longer hours than any other occupational group, and often suffer from role-overload, resentment, and emotional and physical exhaustion. Rice (1979) regards such role strain of wives as a major source of the marital stress experienced by dual-career couples, while Goldenberg & Goldenberg (1984) suggest that a major conflict to be resolved is ''how best to get beyond the traditional sex roles, especially in regard to domestic duties'' (p. 30).

## Conflict Over Structuring and Managing Time

Managing time is another key area of stress for dual-career couples. The multitude of in- and out-of-home responsibilities allow little time for spontaneity or unscheduled leisure and make a formal schedule mandatory (Rice, 1979, p. 56). Couples must learn to respect each other's priorities and to co-operate in organizing their schedules so they can arrange for time alone and together as well as for time with their children (Goldenberg & Goldenberg, 1984). Rapoport and Rapoport (1976) emphasize the importance of both husbands and wives spending less time at work and giving more time to their relationship.

## Frustration of Dependency Needs

Related to problems of structuring role responsibilities and managing time is what Bird (1979, p. 232) has called the "Bind of the Two Person Career"—i.e., the lack of an unofficial "Second Person" to provide the backup and behind-the-scenes support which career men have ordinarily received from their wives. Dual-career spouses may feel that their partner is not backing them up or taking care of them sufficiently, and the resulting frustration of dependency needs may lead them to invest more in their careers than in the marriage (Rice, 1979, p. 3).

## Competition

A fourth major area where dual-career couples experience stress is in competition between the spouses (Rapoport & Rapoport, 1969, 1976; Shaevitz & Shaevitz, 1980). Rice (1979) suggests that "competitive feelings related to each other's careers are natural and inevitable" (p. 75) for most dual-career couples, partly because of their high achievement needs. Admitting and facing such feelings is the first step to learning how to deal with them. If couples deny their competitive feelings, they will tend to express them indirectly, in ways that are harmful to the relationship. Such competition may take the form of conflict over whose career/time is more important than whose, and is directly related to the distribution and balance of power between the couple. Because women typically assume more responsibility for home and parenting than their husbands, they also typically achieve less in their careers (Bryson, Bryson, Licht & Licht, 1976). If a wife perceives of herself as making more sacrifices for the marriage or family than her husband, and of his career consequently advancing more quickly at the expense of hers, the result may be greater resentment, conflict and competition (Goldenberg & Goldenberg, 1984; Rice, 1979). Rice states that "for many career women the sum total of gains and losses simply does not balance out fairly" (p. 76). Consequently, he suggests that the most important single goal, the "guiding principle" in work with dual-career couples, is "to help partners achieve or restore a sense of equity in the marital relationship" (p. 103). This is the underlying goal of the enrichment program presented here.

## THE ENRICHMENT PROGRAM

The situation confronting dual-career couples, then, is one in which they have chosen a lifestyle which is different from their parents', for which they have no blueprint, and for which they have been ill-prepared by their gender-role socialization. This enrichment program responds to the needs of such couples for learning the attitudes and skills necessary to cope effectively with their lifestyle. It is based on the assumption that a sense of inequity or imbalance in power and responsibility is destructive to dual-career marriages, and achieving an equalitarian balance is thus its major underlying goal. Achieving such a balance involves reexamining assumptions and beliefs regarding "appropriate" male and female roles, renegotiating expectations, roles and responsibilities in the home, and working co-operatively and supportively to effect change.

The program is intended to be used as a guide for leaders designing programs for this population. It is designed around the needs which have been found to be most general and frequent among dual-career couples and may be expanded, reduced or otherwise altered in order to tailor it to the needs of a specific group. The program may also be adapted to the needs of two-worker couples, but because of differences between these two groups, especially in the wife's power in the relationship, it is recommended that the participants in any one group share a common lifestyle.

### Program Goals

The program attempts to enable dual-career couples to:

1. Examine their values and priorities concerning work and family;
2. Examine their present allocations of roles and responsibilities and determine how effective and appropriate they are in terms of their current life situation;
3. Become more aware of the influence of their gender-role socialization on both their present division of roles and tasks, as well as on the options and choices they consider;
4. Identify attitudes, beliefs and behaviors which create barriers to change, and develop ones which are more facilitative;

5. Become aware of new options and choices;
6. Develop the communication and negotiation skills, as well as the spirit of cooperation and flexible attitudes necessary for planning change;
7. Develop a support system for exploring these life-style and equity issues with couples experiencing similar life situations.

## *Group Preparation*

The program is intended for four to six non-clinical couples. All applicant couples are asked to complete an application form (on a brochure) indicating their reasons for wishing to attend and what they hope to gain, both individually and as a couple, from participating. Wherever possible, they are asked to meet with one or both leaders to discuss the purposes and goals of the group and to mutually determine its appropriateness to their needs. Where this is not practical, a telephone interview may be used instead, but this is considered less satisfactory. The interview is an aid to leaders in building rapport with participants, obtaining information concerning their needs which will be useful in designing the program, and screening out deeply troubled couples for whom therapy would be more appropriate. Each participant is asked to read *The Two-Paycheck Marriage* (Bird, 1979) prior to beginning the program. This is an aid both to normalizing this family form, and to stimulating participants' thinking regarding creative problem-solving.

## *Format and Structure*

The workshop is held in seven weekly two-and-a-half hour evening sessions in a comfortable lounge which is both pleasant and private. It is important that chairs be easily movable and that there be space for couples to spread out for private discussions. Sessions are limited both in number and length to accommodate the severe time constraints of dual-career couples.

Group sessions are designed to allow maximum participation within a structured format. Structure is deemed essential in order to reduce anxiety and ensure that involvement is goal-directed. Variety in the type and pace of activities helps to keep participants stimulated and to enable learning to take place on many different levels—cognitively, emotionally, and behaviorally. Each session begins with a brief "community time", which allows unstructured time for participants to raise questions, concerns or learnings occurring since the last session. This is followed by some combination of structured experiences, mini-lectures, skill practice, couple and group discussions designed to meet the session objectives.

Sessions are designed to respond directly to issues raised by participants during the pre-workshop interview and during the first session.

Although leadership ideally is provided by a dual-career therapist couple, it may also be provided by an unmarried male and female therapist team, or by a single leader working alone. As Goldenberg & Goldenberg (1984) point out, "probably the most important consideration for the therapist working with . . . dual-career couples is that he or she has worked out his or her own personal solutions to these issues" (p. 36). It is considered imperative that the leader[s] be part of a dual-career family and thus have personal understanding of the stresses and problems which are part of this lifestyle. Because of the nature of the exploration of gender role issues in this program, a male-female team (whether married or not) is considered most effective in giving support to both genders as they explore these emotionally-laden issues.

A warm, safe, friendly, and non-defensive atmosphere is promoted in every way possible—by the physical environment, informality of sessions, leaders' positive and encouraging attitudes, and the provision of helpful ground rules. Coffee and hot chocolate are available before and during each session to contribute to informality and comfort.

### Session 1: Getting Started—Introduction and Goals

*Objectives*

1. To meet group inclusion and acceptance needs (Schutz, 1973) and help participants become oriented to the group;
2. To identify individual, couple and group goals;
3. To establish ground rules;
4. To clarify roles of leaders and participants.

*Procedures*

1. Introduction. The leaders welcome participants, congratulating them for their interest in exploring new ways of working together and their willingness to risk change. They briefly introduce the program, give an overview of the evening, and outline the ground rules. These include respecting confidentiality, speaking for oneself, sharing air time, avoiding psychologizing or advice giving, freedom to not participate in any exercise or activity, starting and stopping on time.
2. Introductions reflect the program emphasis on both individuals and couples. Each person takes two to three minutes to introduce him or herself to the group and to share several things they would like the group to know about them. Each couple then shares how and when

they became a dual-career couple. The leaders model the process by introducing themselves first.
3. Men's and women's groups. The group is divided by gender and each group asked to identify the costs and benefits *for their gender* of being a dual-career couple. Each group records their findings on newsprint and appoints a spokesperson who reports their findings to the total group.
4. Break
5. Identifying strengths and goals.
   a. Each couple meets alone to discuss their strengths as a couple as well as areas they want to change or work on during the workshop.
   b. Each couple shares with another couple their major strengths and areas of stress.
   c. In the large group, each couple shares one or two of their strengths and one or two of their goals. The leaders record these strengths and goals on sheets of newsprint (one for each couple) which they have posted on the wall. These sheets are saved and hung on the wall during future sessions.
6. Group contract. Leaders ask participants what they need from themselves, their partners, the group and the leaders in order to meet their goals. This affords a good opportunity for issues of self-responsibility, risk, cooperation and mutal support to be discussed.
7. Overview of the program. Leaders give a more detailed overview of the focus and format of future sessions, emphasizing how the program will respond to the needs and goals identified by the couples. They also emphasize the usefulness of "homework" and non-usefulness of "right-wrong" or "win-lose" thinking in effecting change.
8. Closing. The session ends with a sentence completion exercise (adapted from Simon, Howe & Kirschenbaum, 1972, p. 162), with participants reflecting on their experience during the evening by completing any of the following statements that the leaders have written on newsprint: "Tonight I learned that . . .", "Tonight I relearned that . . .", "Tonight I noticed that . . .", "Tonight I realized that . . .", "Tonight I was pleased that . . .", etc.

### Session 2: Talking Together

*Objectives*

To increase partners' skills in:

1. Expressing thoughts, feelings, perceptions, intentions, expectations, needs and wants in personally responsible ways;

2. Listening accurately, attentively and empathically;
3. Active listening and paraphrasing;
4. Checking out the meaning of messages by reflecting back verbally what has been heard (Miller, Nunnally & Wackman, 1975).

*Procedures*

1. Community time. Participants are invited to share any thoughts, feelings, concerns or learnings which have arisen since the last session. This is also the time when "housekeeping" issues such as coffee, leaving the room tidy, etc., may be discussed.
2. The leaders give a brief mini-lecture on effective communication and its importance in developing and maintaining satisfying marital relationships. Its particular importance in dual-career marriages, where socialized expectations often do not fit reality, is emphasized. A chart of the Awareness Wheel (Miller, Nunnally & Wackman, 1979) is used to demonstrate the interplay of sensing, thinking, feeling, intending and acting in all communication. The levels of communication (process/content; verbal/nonverbal; cognitive/affective) and the basic rules for both speaking and listening roles are outlined and demonstrated. (See Hof & Miller, 1981, pp. 87–89 for a useful outline.) Finally, those areas of communication which tend to be more problematic for each gender are pointed out (e.g., "I feel" statements for men and "I think, believe, want" statements for women).
3. Skills practice.

   a. *Individually*—Each person completes, four times, in writing, the following sentence in relation to their partner. Two of the sentences should express positive feelings and two, negative ones:
   "When I notice (perceive, observe, see) you. . . . , I think (interpret). . . . and I feel. . . . ".
   b. *With partner*—Partners sit face-to-face, with knees touching, and maintaining eye contact. One begins by stating the first of his or her *positive* feeling sentences. The other paraphrases what they have heard and checks out to ensure that they have understood the message accurately. When the first agrees that they have been understood, the couple switches roles. They continue to alternate speaking and listening roles until they have communicated all of their sentences to each other, starting with the positive ones. When finished, they discuss their feelings about the exercise and which parts of the communication process they found easiest and most difficult.

c. *With another couple*—Each couple pairs with another and shares their feelings about the exercise and the areas they found easy and difficult. Each person speaks for him or herself.

4. Break
5. Mini-lecture on the difference between wants and needs (Hof & Miller, 1981, pp. 99–100). Wants are considered to be those things which are strongly desired, but not considered absolutely essential, in the marital relationship, while needs are those things considered absolutely necessary for the continuation of the relationship.
6. *Skills practice* in expressing wants and needs (based on Hof & Miller, 1981, pp. 100).

   a. *Individually*—Each person is asked to make two lists in their own notebook—one of their wants and one of their needs in the marriage relationship. They are asked to indicate beside each need and want whether or not it is presently being fully or partly met in the relationship. Each person is then asked to identify at least one specific way in which they would like a want or need to be different (e.g., to reorganize parenting responsibilities so they are more evenly shared), as well as what they are prepared to do to help bring about that change.
   b. *With Partner*—Partners share their lists with each other, with the emphasis on sharing and understanding, not on reaching agreement or planning for change.

7. *Group reflection.* The total group reflects on their learnings from the evening by making "I" statements about the experience. Couples are asked to practice their speaking and listening skills during the week, but to not yet attempt to negotiate change.

### Session 3: Gender Socialization and Us (or, "Roles We Have Learned")

*Objectives*

1. To help spouses become more aware of the impact of gender socialization on their beliefs, expectations, roles and choices;
2. To identify spouses' role expectations, and differences in expectation, both of themselves and of each other;
3. To help couples become aware of their initial ("unwritten") marital contract and to construct a new one which more accurately reflects their current relationship.

*Procedures*

1. Community time.
2. Warm-up exercise. A values exercise which focuses on beliefs about gender roles is used to introduce the subject and stimulate thinking and discussion. Signs are hung on different walls, designating "strongly agree", "agree", "disagree", "strongly disagree". The leaders then read out a list of value statements, one at a time. Participants go to the sign which best fits their response to the statement. They then discuss their choice with others who have the same response. Statements such as "Whichever spouse earns the most should have the final say in money matters"; "Housework is primarily a woman's responsibility"; "Mothers are better able than fathers to nurture children"; "When a child is sick, it makes more sense for mother than for father to stay home"; "A wife should be willing to move when her husband's career demands it"; "A husband should be willing to move when his wife's career demands it". The exercise is followed by brief group discussion.
3. The process and impact of gender-role socialization.

    a. *Mini-lecture.* This includes discussion of the deeply held, emotionally laden beliefs about "appropriate" roles and responsibilities for men and women, how gender-role socialization occurs, and the ways in which it is different for girls and boys. The leaders briefly present research findings on the negative impact of stereotyped roles for all family members, as well as the special hazards of role strain for dual-career wives, and thus for dual-career couples.

    b. *Men's and women's groups.* Each gender group is asked to discuss and list on newsprint the things they were taught (by parents, teachers, church, media) about what it is to be a real man or a real woman.

    c. *Group discussion.* Each gender group reports their findings. The whole group then examines which beliefs are out-dated and hinder change, and explores alternative beliefs which promote flexibility and innovation and thus facilitate change.

4. Break
5. Marital Contract exercise (see Rice, 1979, p. 104, and Sager, 1976).

    a. *Individually*—Each person writes down in their own notebook their expectations of their partner and of themselves at the time of their marriage.

    b. *With Partner*—Spouses share their initial expectations and discuss their initial "unwritten" contract.

c. *Individually*—Each person writes down their present expectations of themselves, their partner and the relationship.

d. *With Partner*—Spouses share their present expectations and relationship goals, noting areas of agreement and disagreement. They begin to write a single, mutual contract composed of the expectations and goals they agree upon.

6. Group discussion. Group members reflect on the experience of identifying expectations and re-writing their marital contracts. They share areas of success as well as difficulty. The session ends with instructions to couples to continue discussing their contracts at home.

### Session 4: Power and Control—How Can We Share It?

*Objectives*

1. To review couples' initial goals for the workshop and assess their progress towards meeting them.
2. To increase spouses' understanding of issues of power and control in marriage relationships;
3. To help spouses examine the division of power in their own relationship and renegotiate areas of disagreement.

*Procedures*

1. Community time.
2. Review of goals exercise.

   a. *With Partner:* Each couple reviews their original goals for the workshop and discusses their progress towards meeting them. They either reaffirm their goals or develop new ones for the remainder of the program, and discuss the steps they will take to accomplish them.

   b. *With Another Couple:* Each couple shares with another couple their reactions to the program so far as well as their progress in meeting their goals.

   c. *With Group:* The total group meets and briefly discusses where individuals and couples are at the halfway point in the group, as well as hopes, fears and expectations for the remainder of the program.

3. Mini-lecture on power issues in marriage, including needs for control, direct and indirect control, decision-making and power, issues related to gender and power, and the relationships between level of income and level of power, and between competitiveness

and power imbalance. Examples are given of exercise of power, and the importance of establishing a sense of equity for both partners is emphasized.

4. Break.
5. Who Makes the Decisions? Exercise.

   a. *Individually:* Each spouse is asked to fill out a decision-making chart indicating who makes the decisions (always husband, usually husband, usually shared, usually wife, always wife) in a variety of areas (how money is spent, where the family lives, whether the family moves, who stays home when a child is ill, who does the housework, etc.) They are asked to note how it is now, and how they would like it to be.
   b. *With Partner:* Spouses share and compare their answers and identify areas of agreement and disagreement, regarding both how decisions are made now, and how they would like them to be made in the future. Spouses use their speaking and listening skills to understand each other's feelings and point of view and to discuss specifically how they want to change the balance of power in their relationship so that it feels equitable to both partners.
   c. *With Another Couple:* Couples share with one other couple any changes they plan to make in the balance of power.

6. Group reflection on learnings from evening.
7. Homework. Couples are asked to make a ''responsibility chart'' at home during the week in preparation for the next session (Lederer & Jackson, 1968). This is a master list which the couple composes of all tasks and responsibilities in the family, listed under four headings, according to who takes responsibility for seeing that they are done: husband, wife, both, neither. They are asked to bring their charts to the next session.

## Session 5—Negotiating Responsibilities

*Objectives*

1. To help couples examine their present distribution of roles and responsibilities and determine whether it meets present needs;
2. To help couples identify any traps or problematic solutions they may be using in trying to manage a multiplicity of roles.

*Procedures*

1. Community time.
2. Sharing responsibilities.

a. *Mini-lecture*. This talk ties together issues of gender socialization and power distribution with the way in which parenting and domestic responsibilities are shared (or not shared) in the marriage. The research findings that most working women continue to have primary responsibility for children and home and thus have the longest work week of any occupational group is pointed out, as well as the implications of this arrangement for dual-career couples in terms of lack of felt equity and development of resentment.

b. *With Partner:* Each couple discusses together their own responsibility chart, using the Awareness Wheel and active listening to share perceptions, thoughts, and feelings about how their responsibilities are presently distributed. Each is asked to state what he/she would be willing to do to help areas of difficulty go more smoothly and to achieve a more equitable distribution.

c. *With Another Couple:* Each couple shares with another couple the changes they intend to make. Each person speaks for him/herself.

3. Break.
4. Mini-lecture on some of the most common pitfalls for dual-career couples, including superwomen, perfectionism, believing one must do it all oneself, feeling competitive with one's partner's career, feeling resentful at one's lack of a "Second Person", etc. (see Bird, 1979, for a helpful elaboration of many of these). Each of these pitfalls is described, as well as their consequences.
5. Men's and women's groups. The group is divided by gender and each subgroup is asked to identify and discuss the pitfalls they most commonly fall into, and the consequences. They are then asked to discuss alternatives to these traps and to record their main findings on newsprint.
6. Group discussion. Each gender group reports their findings to the total group and the group reflects on learning about structuring responsibilities.

### Session 6: Managing Time

### Objectives

1. To enable couples to examine the way in which they presently divide and spend their time, and to determine to what degree this fits with what they believe is important in their lives;
2. To encourage couples to plan for time alone together and increase their ability to do so.

*Procedures*

1. Community time.
2. Warm-up exercise. A values exercise focusing on how people prefer to spend their time. Participants are asked to indicate their answers to a series of choices (e.g., "Would you rather read a book or lie on a beach?") by going to one end of the room or the other and briefly discussing their choice with someone who made the same choice.
3. Mini-lecture on time. This includes issues around values and time, managing time, and the different kinds of time needed in a marriage (alone, couple, family, and recreation times).
4. Time Inventories (Josofowitz, 1979).

   a. *Individually:* Participants are given a sheet containing two blank circles. They are asked to divide the first into wedges corresponding to the amount of time they spend in various activities during a typical day (working, parenting, homemaking, playing, recreating, eating, sleeping, time alone with spouse, time alone, etc.). The second circle is then divided according to how they would *like* to spend their time.

   b. *With Partner:* Spouses share their charts, using their speaking and listening skills to reach a shared understanding. Each person tells their partner two things they would be willing to do to bring their ideal time charts more in line with each other, particularly in the areas of individual, couple and family time.

5. Break.
6. Planning Quality Time Exercise. Each couple lists and discusses ways of spending some quality time together each week. They are then asked to develop a plan for spending some time alone together during the coming week and to make a commitment to carrying it out. Finally, they meet with another couple to outline their plan.
7. Group reflection on learnings and sharing of plans.

### Session 7: Termination

*Objectives*

1. To help couples identify change and growth in their relationship as well as future work areas;
2. To terminate the group.

*Procedures*

1. Community time.

2. Mini-lecture on consolidating and maintaining change. Issues such as slumps, slip-backs, and dealing with negative reactions of family and friends to change are discussed.
3. Collage. Working together, each couple makes a drawing or collage of where their relationship was, where it is now, and the direction they would like it to take in the future. A variety of materials are supplied for this exercise, including magazines, crayons, colored pens, bits of fabric and yarn, glue, and sheets of newsprint. When finished, each couple briefly shares their collage and its meaning with the total group. Each couple is allowed a maximum of five minutes, and the time limits are strictly enforced with the use of a timer.
4. Couple Contracts. Using their collage to identify where they want their relationship to go, each spouse tells their partner what he or she intends to do to help this to happen. Each puts his/her own commitment in writing, on a single sheet of paper, and they then share this commitment with one other couple.
5. Break.
6. Affirmation exercise. Partners alternate with each other completing a number of sentences which focus on the strengths and positives in their relationship (e.g., "I love you because . . . ", "I appreciate you when you . . . ", "I feel loved when you . . . ", etc.).
7. Workshop evaluation—written and verbal.
8. Group hug and farewells.

## CONCLUSION

"Working Together" is a newly-developed program which is offered as a possible guideline to enrichment leaders wishing to work with dual-career couples. The program is still in the developmental stage and further research will be necessary to fully evaluate its effectiveness. As part of this evaluation, comments and feedback from readers who implement all or parts of the program will be welcomed.

Some type of self-report form completed by participants at completion of the program is a useful way of obtaining feedback on a number of dimensions. Success in obtaining completed forms seems much greater if time is allowed during the final session for completing them, as opposed to participants taking forms home and mailing them back.

One way of collecting feedback is the following: On the final evening, each couple is given back their original application form, containing their initial statements of both couple and individual goals for the workshop. Each person is asked to evaluate, in writing, the extent to which the program enabled them to meet their couple and individual goals, and to comment specifically on the usefulness of each session as well as on various aspects of the program. A combination of closed and open-ended questions are used, including questions about what specific changes/ improvements in their marriage have occurred as a result of the workshop, and their suggestions for modifications in the program.

The generalizability of the program across ages, socio-economic groups and occupations has not been tested. Although many of the issues addressed are also relevant to two income couples where neither, or only the husband, is professionally employed, these couples tend to be more traditional than dual-career couples in terms of their attitudes about the equalization of power and the division of domestic responsibilities (Goldenberg & Goldenberg, 1984). Since they tend not to be committed, even in belief, to an egalitarian division of roles, and since these wives usually have much lower incomes than their husbands, and thus much less power in the marriage, the program would have to be adjusted to respond effectively to the value system these couples present.

As the numbers of dual-career couples continue to increase, therapists and enrichment leaders are likely to be increasingly called upon to help these couples make the adjustments and accommodations required by their particular family structure. "Working Together" is presented as an enrichment program designed to facilitate this process of reevaluation and learning.

## REFERENCES

Bird, C. (1979). *The two-paycheck marriage.* NY: Pocket Books.
Bryson, R. B., Bryson, J. B., Licht, M. H. & Licht, B. G. (1976). The professional pair: Husband and wife psychologists. *American Psychologist, 31,* 10–16.
Goldenberg, I. & Goldenberg, H. (1984). Treating the dual-career couple. *The American Journal of Family Therapy, 12,* 29–37.
Hall, F. S. & Hall, D. T. (1979). *The two-career couple.* Reading, MA: Addison-Wesley.
Hof, L. & Miller, W. R. (1981). *Marriage enrichment: Philosophy, process, & program.* Bowie, MD: Robert J. Brady Co.
Johnson, C. L. & Johnson, F. A. (1977). Attitudes toward parenting in dual-career families. *American Journal of Psychiatry, 134, 4,* 391–395.
Josofowitz, N. (1980). *Paths to Power.* Reading, MA: Addison-Wesley.
Kimball, G. (1983). *The 50.50 marriage.* Boston, MA: Beacon Press.
Lederer, W. J. & Jackson, D. D. (1968). *The mirages of marriage.* NY: W. W. Norton & Co.
Miller, S., Nunnally, E. W., & Wackman, D. B. (1975). *Alive and aware.* Minneapolis: Interpersonal Communication Programs.
Miller, S., Nunnally, E. W., & Wackman, D. B. (1979). *Couple communication I: Talking together.* Minneapolis, Minnesota: Interpersonal Communication Programs, Inc.
Pepitone-Rockwell, F. (Ed.) (1980). *Dual-career couples.* Beverly Hills: Sage.
Rapoport, R. & Rapoport, R. (1969). The dual-career family. *Human Relations, 22,* 3–30.
Rapoport, R. & Rapoport, R. (1976). *Dual-career families re-examined: New integration of work and family.* NY: Harper.
Rice, D. G. (1979). *Dual-career marriage: Conflict and treatment.* NY: The Free Press.
Sager, C. J. (1976). *Marriage contracts and couple therapy.* New York: Brunner/Mazel.
Scanzoni, J. (1978). *Sex roles, women's work and marital conflict.* Toronto: Lexington Books.

Schutz, W. C. (1973). Encounter. In R. Corsini, Ed., *Current psychotherapies*. Itasca, IL: Peacock.

Shaevitz, M. H. & Shaevitz, M. H. (1980). *Making it together as a two-career couple*. Boston: Houghton Mifflin.

Simon, S. B., Howe, L. W., & Kirschenbaum, H. (1972). *Values clarification: A handbook of practical strategies for teachers and students*. NY: Hart Publishing Co.

Stapleton, J. & Bright, R. (1976). *Equal marriage*. Nashville, Tenn.: Abingdon.

Tavris, C. & Wade, C. (1984). *The longest war: Sex differences in perspective* (2nd ed.). NY: Harcourt Brace Jovanovich.

# The Family Cluster Approach to Family Enrichment

Margaret M. Sawin

**ABSTRACT.** This article covers the history of enrichment and place of the Family Cluster Model within that movement. It is suggested as a preventive mode which emphasizes the total family system as a means of learning and growth. Descriptive characteristics of the Family Cluster are given along with the composition of a session with families. This is followed by presentation of the theoretical foundations of the model. Adaptations, as well as limitations, are included, as well as information given for further reading.

The concept of enrichment, as a form of primary prevention, is now being accepted by many professional groups. It has yet to be widely instituted in human service agencies because of the difficulty in "selling" programs of enrichment. People follow society's norms in waiting for dysfunction to take over before seeking help; therefore, education and prevention for interpersonal family relations is a new concept to be furthered with the American public.

This article presents a primary preventive model, known as the Family Cluster, and how it has facilitated family living for the past fifteen years. It is the oldest model of family enrichment, as well as the one most extensively used in the United States, Canada, New Zealand, Australia and with the United States military forces in Europe.

## HISTORY OF ENRICHMENT

David Mace (1979) has written extensively about enrichment, having developed marriage enrichment with healthy couples during the 1960's, in contrast to his counseling practice with dysfunctioning couples. According to Mace, the basic meaning of enrichment as it relates to the new movement is:

. . . to improve the quality of whatever is already there, latent and

Margaret M. Sawin, EdD, is a consultant in family enrichment and education to religious and community groups. Her address is: Family Clusters, Inc., Box 18452, Rochester, NY 14618.

hitherto unappropriated, and allowing it to function. It is closely related to the concept of realizing potential. It may also be seen as achieving an optimal state of health. (p. 409)

## Individual Enrichment

Abraham Maslow (1962) popularized the concept of individual enrichment within modern psychology. He stressed that the norms, for what constituted a normal individual, should be developed from the observation of healthy persons, rather than dysfunctional ones. Thus, the foundation for health and wholeness was established as the basis for growing and maturing, encouraging a holistic manner of perceiving persons.

## Marriage Enrichment

In 1962 David and Vera Mace began the concept of marriage or couple enrichment within the United States. They were interested in the family's well-being and thought that the parental couple's relationship was the crucial factor in total family health. Using a group approach, they introduced experiential techniques, linked with didactic input, to groups of couples who wanted to build stronger marriages.

About the same time the Maces were working in the United States, Father Gabriel Calvo was pondering the nature of healthy family life within his Catholic parish in Barcelona, Spain. Like the Maces, he decided that the marital dyad was the crucial factor and needed strengthening to meet its task of undergirding the family. Calvo developed the model known as "Marriage Encounter" which consists of written dialogues in an intentional format between the spouses.

In 1978 Mace wrote that approximately a million couples had been involved in some form of family enrichment. By now there must be close to two million couples who have enhanced their marital dyads through numerous models of marriage and family enrichment.

## Parent-Child Enrichment

Americans have some history of parent study groups, but Thomas Gordon (1970) popularized the concept with the introduction of his skill-based program entitled, *Parent Effectiveness Training.* "To fix up one's child" is a constant concern of parents, so parent-child enrichment is considered one of the easiest forms to attract people. Other models have been developed and are used widely in many communities.

*Total Family Enrichment*

In 1970 Margaret Sawin developed the Family Cluster in Rochester, N.Y., as a way for the total family system to learn together in order to enhance family living. The model was developed in response to a concern that the religious education programs in most congregations were built on peer groupings whereby the family unit was divided by ages for its religious instruction. Churches and synagogues did not consider parents as teachers in the process of faith development; their job simply was to send children to church school or CCD (Confraternity of Christian Doctrine) where they would be taught the fundamentals of the faith. The everyday life of parents, as models for faith living, was not considered. Sawin was convinced that a stronger means of relating religious thought and practice would take place if family members were together in learning groups. In our society, religious institutions are the only ones which have the complete family within their clientele and where all generations are involved; therefore, they provide a natural place in which to work preventively with families.

About the same time, Herbert Otto (1971) developed a similar model on the west coast, calling it by the same name of Family Cluster. However, since it was not affiliated with an existing institution, Otto's model has been in decline since the 1970's. There appears to be a correlation between the development of family groups and existing institutional strength. Since there are few societal organizations to which the complete family belongs, there are few common loyalties families can use to strengthen themselves.

Since the mid-seventies, there has been a steady increase in the recognition of the movement defined as "enrichment." In 1975, the term, "Family Cluster" became an integral listing in *The Reader's Guide to Periodical Literature.* In 1976 the first workshop on total family enrichment was introduced at the annual conference of The American Association for Marriage and Family Therapy. In 1980 the membership of The National Council on Family Relations instituted a section for persons involved in enrichment forms, indicating it was a new field of professional involvement. Perhaps enrichment has come of age!

## THE FAMILY CLUSTER MODEL

Since the Family Cluster was the first model developed in total family enrichment, the term has been used often as a generic one until it was defined in the first book written on the subject by Sawin (1979):

A Family Cluster is a group of four or five complete family units which contract to meet together periodically over an extended period of time for shared educational experiences related to living in relationship within their families. A Cluster provides mutual support, training in skills which facilitate family living, and celebration of their life and beliefs together. A family unit may be composed of any persons who live in relationship with one another. (p. 27)

From this definition, one can see that there are three basic components to the group process of clustering:

1. Support and caring are given to families, as units. There are few situations in our culture where complete family units are affirmed and supported for what they are. This includes all kinds of family life styles, i.e., single parent families, blended families, those without children, etc. Observation of different ways of living as well as modeling for each other become powerful tools of teaching, showing a manner of care, and sustenance.

2. The learning and practicing of relational skills is emphasized as a means for families to facilitate each other as well as their system. There are no courses in our society where mixed ages of people are taught competency in the use of interpersonal skills, yet these are the way that intimacy needs are met adequately. In Family Cluster, skills are taught according to the families' needs and desires, as they grow in awareness of what will help their systems to become more actualized. Communication and decision-making skills seem to be the ones most desired by beginning clusters.

Experience with clusters suggests that families need to develop a great deal of trust among themselves before they are willing to move into the more difficult areas of use of anger, conflict resolution, and re-negotiation.

3. The celebration of family rituals are fostered as a means of faith growth. The diminishing acts of ritualizing and celebrating have made us aware of their importance in family living. Family therapist, Edwin Friedman (1980) has written that the periods of familial interaction surrounding rites of passage are the "hinges of time," marking transitions from one period of the family life cycle to the next. Thus, they signify a strong opportunity for change within a family system. The church and synagogue are the societal institutions which use ritual and liturgy to mark family transitions, i.e. marriage, baptism at birth, confirmation at puberty, and death. Today, many religious institutions have added new rituals to mark the transitions of divorce and re-marriage.

# WHAT IS A CLUSTER LIKE?

Recruitment of families is initiated through publicity which is followed by the leader's visits to the homes of interested families. At that time an informal contract or agreement is made with *all* family members to attend regularly ten to twelve sessions of a cluster group. It has been found that fewer sessions do not seem to be effective in helping a group build trust in order to accomplish family change. Therefore, it is important to have the complete family knowledgeable about the importance of their attendance at all sessions. This act is unusual in our society inasmuch as we are not accustomed to the family agreeing and then participating as a unit in a growth group over a period of time.

When the cluster begins with families who have been contacted in the above manner, a high degree of motivation is already present. The first three sessions are devoted to getting acquainted, group-building, and group contracting. This entails outlining of expectations, agreements on time scheduling and use of space, plus ways decisions will be made. How persons will interact with each other is also considered in light of the intimacy of the family, as well as ways the contract can be renegotiated. Everyone shares in the development of the contract, making that the "gem" of the cluster concept, according to sociologist Sangree (1974).

After the beginning sessions of group consolidation, the desires and interests of the families become the agenda for ongoing sessions. Terminating the cluster is usually accomplished in the last two sessions while some clusters recontract for additional sessions. Accounts of various types of clusters, as well as long-term ones, are found in Sawin (1982) *Hope for Families*.

An individual session, built on learning objectives around a common theme, is composed of the following:

1. Pre-session activities while families gather.
2. A simple meal with each family bringing its own food.
3. Group time with sharing of concerns, singing, announcements, etc.
4. Fun and recreation.
5. The major structured learning experience, based on families' desires and their ages, as planned by the co-leaders.
6. Evaluation and closure.

These activities usually take place within a two to three hour span, depending on the time of day and ages of family members. Detailed information about cluster sessions and activities used are available in Sawin (1979) *Family Enrichment with Family Clusters*, as well as Sawin (1982) *Hope for Families*.

## THEORETICAL FOUNDATIONS OF THE
## FAMILY CLUSTER MODEL

There are five synthesizing components which provide theoretical undergirding to the model. These areas of knowledge and related research contribute to the philosophical foundations of how it works.

### The Family as a System

The basic premise which provides the *foundation* for the model is that the system of the family can provide its own intensive framework for growth when set within the wider context of the cluster system. Activities emphasize family strengths, so their inter-relational systems can be recognized and used as a springboard for further growth. By exposing all family members together in a learning situation, each is influenced by his or her own perceptual framework, by the others, and by the unit as a whole. This kind of teaching makes for more potency than an individual style, as attested by the authors of the book, *No Single Thread* (Lewis et al., 1976) who say, " . . . the systems approach was more apt to reveal the strengths of a family while the individual, 'composite' approach . . . more often highlighted the family problem" (p. 204). It is as though the exponential influence escalates for positive growth.

### The Group Process

The *strength* of the Family Cluster is derived from the group which develops mutual support and gives feedback to family members and units. Because the cluster may be composed of differing family life styles, members can observe other family units in various experiences of communication, decision making, and problem solving. In a time of rapid social change, it becomes imperative that we find ways for people to adapt, to cope, and to share intimacies in the midst of differing value systems from those with which they grew up. Each individual is respected and important to the life of the group, whether child, adolescent, or adult. Each has an opportunity to be "teacher" as well as "learner" which avoids the hierarchical structure where only adults are teachers.

A developing group has certain dynamics at work between its members and its subsystem, which in this case are family systems. This makes the ground rules considerably different from those in a group composed of individual peers. In this capacity, the Family Cluster presents a uniqueness to the group work movement.

There is intra-family exchange as well as inter-family exchange, which helps the cluster become often like an extended family. One of the original groups, started in 1970, met for five years and still has a yearly "reunion," while the families still maintain contact with each other. The stress of parenting, coupled with environmental pressures, makes family support groups essential for today's functional living.

## Change and Growth

The *outcome* of the Family Cluster is intentional change, followed by growth which leads toward fulfillment of actualization. Families are encouraged to discover their latent resources and to experiment with new behaviors, which offer more options and choices in a fast-paced world. This approach empowers both individuals and units so they are able to cope more effectively with crises.

Hunsicker (1982) has written how the cluster group also becomes a system which lends its support to the change/growth process within and between family units. The characteristics of healthy families, toward which growth is directed, come from various studies which have indicated such in recent years (Curran, 1983; Lewis et al., 1976; Stinnett, 1979).

## Experiential Learning

The *method* of achieving growth is that of experiential education where reflecting on one's experiences becomes the "heart" of the learning. Since each is his or her own expert on family life, this provides a ready avenue for learning among all ages.

The content/subject areas are garnered from families in terms of their strengths, concerns, hopes, problems, dreams, and questions. The expression of these is enhanced through the use of subjective techniques, i.e., role play, use of clay, relational exercises, puppetry, games, songs, finger painting. These are not only fun for all ages to use, but germane to the expression of family interests.

After participating in an exercise developed for expressed family needs and designed by the leaders, the group shares in reflection upon the experience. A learning assumption is that, in a cluster setting, learning comes best from reflective evaluation than didactic input. From this point, families may move into discussing and analyzing ways they hope to transfer their new learnings to the family system at home.

Most clusters meet in church settings where there is a shared meeting space. Younger children have a play corner to which they are free to move, if desired. Often the play reflects the emotional dynamics and content of the group. There is a definite movement between child play and concerns of the larger group which make it an emotional barometer for how the group is reacting.

*Existential Valuing/Process Theologizing*

The *interpretation* of these experiences is done through the medium of existential valuing known as "Process" or "Relational Theology" in religious circles. Lived experiences are considered in terms of values clarifying practices or "reverential thinking" (Yankelovich, 1981). Since all of life's experiences can have sacred interpretation, every occasion becomes a setting for learning about one's life within the ultimate of a Higher Being. The basic elements of any belief—trust, autonomy, initiative, integrity, stewardship—are built out of the psychodynamics of interpersonal relationships which receive their greatest impact from the family (Rizzuto, 1979). It is no coincidence that in studies of functioning or healthy families, one aspect which appears is a high degree of religious orientation (Stinnett, 1979).

Today there is desperate need for a neutral, but respected, meeting ground where valuing issues and faith stances can be considered and from which intentionalized decisions may be made for the good of the system. Buckland (1982) suggests that when all family members participate together in the sharing of selves, behavioral change is accelerated in the intentional direction.

## ADAPTATIONS OF THE MODEL

Because the Family Cluster is a process-oriented model, it lends itself to wide adaptations. Since the families determine the agenda, it is amenable to wide cultural patterns and various targeted populations. Often the model has been adapted to fit a limited time span or the sub-systems of a particular group. Some adaptations are with single parent families, mental health units, public schools, military populations, prisoners and their families, seminarians and lay deacons in training, clergy families, families which have individuals with disabilities, families of adolescents referred by the courts, migrant families, families where children are in residential treatment centers, families caught up with holiday pressures.

In our society, a growing number of families live on the border of crisis but have not yet succumbed to failure. Often they have lost their interpersonal connections, but could be able to "turn the tide" if shown support and better ways of relating. Family sociologist, William Goode (1964), calls them "empty-shell families." Parenting is a lonely task, and the wider society emphasizes competition and individualism to the point of alienation. Family Clustering counteracts these tendencies by establishing a supportive network of care giving to adults, adolescents, and children. This is well described in Brillinger's (1982) account of using the Family Cluster in a Toronto Child and Family Clinic. He has used it with families who were identified as "troubled" and were either awaiting entry into therapy or continuing treatment. As a result, he states, "To date, the evidence suggests that the cluster weekends definitely enhance self-esteem of family members, increase communication skills, lead to positions of greater equality in the family and facilitate collective ability to solve family problems in constructive ways" (p. 189).

To date there has been no statistical research done on the Family Cluster Model. A number of doctoral and master's theses, mostly in theological settings, have been written using a descriptive approach.


## LIMITATIONS TO FAMILY ENRICHMENT


There are some limitations to family enrichment approaches which are not inherent in the models themselves but in the society in which these models are experienced. Some limitations center on myths about the family: fear of loss of privacy and of the discovery of family inadequacies. Discovering other families have like concerns can do much to relieve family members of anxiety. Another limitation is the difficulty of getting all family members together over a period of time, i.e., twelve sessions. In our fragmented society, some groups find they can more easily recruit families over a weekend, but sometimes this becomes prohibitive because of the costs at a retreat center. There is also a limited definition of the term "family" which appears to put a restraint on ready acceptance of other family life styles. Much interpretation of changing norms needs to be offered when recruiting families.

There is also a misunderstanding of "family health" and how it might be measured. Sometimes the concept of perfection is mistaken for health! Trust in the personhood of the leaders is vital. This relates to their humanness, the style of leadership evidenced, and decisions about the degree to which a family might share within the group. The use of a contract which emphasizes modes of interaction and decision-making mitigates for the development of trust and sharing of power.

In American society there are no institutions responsible for the ongoing of healthy family life; therefore, no one helps families to consider what areas they might find helpful in their growth as units. Indeed, there is little to help a family even consider its own evolution toward fulfillment. There is need for training family facilitators who might assist families in their long, hard road to development. Such persons could motivate groups of families to find support, teach skills at necessary points, and help families find adequate ways to ritualize in new life styles. This has been pointed out by Becvar (1985) who assists families, during therapy, to ritualize new transitions in which they are having difficulty.

Family Clustering, Inc., has twelve years' experience in providing skilled leadership throughout the North American Continent. A core of skilled trainers is available for sponsoring agencies who wish to offer training in cluster leadership to their clientele.

## CONCLUSION

Since 1975, there has been a growing number of models within the field of family enrichment, most of which has been in religious settings. However, they reach only those who are members. A vast number of families, unrelated to churches or synagogues, would be touched if such programs were included in the emphases of community agencies. Beavers (1976) states in *No Single Thread* that, " . . . a rapidly adapting family system becomes more of a necessity than a luxury in today's era" (p. 51).

Many families do not need in-depth therapy in order to cope, but they could benefit from added support and skills, buttressed with knowledge, which would make life more productive and joyful. Utilizing enrichment is a way of keeping strong families healthy which, in turn, will make our society more livable. As Uri Bronfenbrenner (1976) has said:

When families become as important to America as football or firearms, the divorce rate will take a deep plunge, non-readers will cease to become a national problem, juvenile delinquency will experience drop-outs, and neighborhoods will once again become a place for people of all ages to live together.

## REFERENCES

Beavers, W.R. (1976). A theoretical basis for family evaluation. In J. M. Lewis, W. R. Beavers, J. T. Gossett & V. A. Phillips, *No Single Thread: Psychological Health in Family Systems* (pp. 46–82). New York: Brunner/Mazel Publishers.

Becvar, D. S. (1985). Creating rituals for a new age: Dealing positively with divorce, remarriage, and other developmental challenges. In N. Stinnett (Ed.), *Family Strengths VI*. Lincoln, NE. University of Nebraska Press.

Brillinger, B. (1982). A mental health experience. In M. Sawin (Ed.), *Hope for Families* (pp. 177–191). New York: William H. Sadlier, Inc.

Bronfenbrenner, U. (1976, November 29). We are not a caring society. *Democrat and Chronicle*, Rochester, NY.

Buckland, C. M. (1972). Toward a theory of parent education: Family living centers in the post-industrialized society. *The Family Coordinator*, *21*(2), 153–160.

Curran, D. (1983). *Traits of a Healthy Family*. Minneapolis, MN: Winston Press.

Friedman, E. H. (1980). Systems and ceremonies: A family view of rites of passage. In E. Carter and M. Goldnick (Eds.), *The Family Life Cycle* (pp. 429–460). New York: Gardner Press.

Good, W. J. (1964). *The Family*. Englewood Cliffs, NJ: Prentice-Hall, Inc.

Gordon, T. (1970). *Parent Effectiveness Training.* New York: Wyden Books.

Hunsicker, R. (1982). Families as systems: The system of the family cluster. In M. Sawin (Ed.), *Hope for Families* (pp. 256–263). New York: William H. Sadlier, Inc.

Lewis, J. M., Beavers, R. W., Gossett, J. R. & Phillips, V. A. (1976). *No Single Threat: Psychological Health in Family Systems.* New York: Brunner/Mazel, Publishers.

Mace, D. & Mace, V. (1978). *The Family Enrichment Center—An Idea Whose Time Has Come.* Unpublished paper for ACME.

Mace, D. (1979). Marriage and family enrichment . . . a new field? *The Family Coordinator, 28*(3), 409–413.

Maslow, A. H. (1962). *Toward a Psychology of Being.* Princeton, NJ: A Van Nostrand Company, Inc.

Otto, H. A. (1971). *The Family Cluster: A Multi-Base Alternative.* Beverly Hills, CA: Holistic Press.

Rizzuto, A. M. (1979). *The Birth of the Living God: A Psychoanalytic Study.* Chicago: The University of Chicago Press.

Sangree, L. (1974). *Report and Evaluation of the Family Cluster Laboratory Process.* Unpublished paper for Family Clustering, Inc.

Sawin, M. M. (1979). *Family Enrichment with Family Clusters.* Valley Forge, PA: Judson Press.

Sawin, M. M. (Ed.). (1982). *Hope for Families.* New York: William H. Sadlier, Inc.

Stinnett, N. (1979). In search of strong families. In N. Stinnett, B. Chesser, J. DeFrain (Eds.), *Building Family Strengths: Blueprints for Action* (pp. 23–30). Lincoln, NB: University of Nebraska Press.

Yankelovich, D. (1981). New rules in American life: Searching for self-fulfillment in a world turned upside down. *Psychology Today, 15*(4), 35–91.

# Structured Enrichment (SE) of a Couple

Frederic E. Stevens
Luciano L'Abate

**ABSTRACT.** This case study illustrates the nature and process of structured enrichment with a couple.

## STRUCTURED ENRICHMENT OF A COUPLE

The wide variety of social skills training programs which are currently available for couples (L'Abate & McHenry, 1983) attest to efforts to develop interventions that are effective and inexpensive. What makes these programs particularly useful is their concern for prevention rather than crisis intervention (Mace, 1983). In these programs, prevention is defined as oriented toward growth with "couples who have what they perceive to be a fairly well functioning marriage and who wish to make their marriages even more naturally satisfying" (Otto, 1976, p. 13). From this perspective (L'Abate, 1985) it is possible to intervene so that couples will not need psychotherapy. For many couples, enrichment may be more appropriate than therapy. Enrichment is also more cost-effective and may be delivered by paraprofessionals. As the delivery of these services relies on subprofessionals and paraprofessionals, it is possible to reach a larger number of couples who need some help but who are not so needy as to require the intervention of a fully trained therapist.

## STRUCTURED ENRICHMENT (SE)

Among various preventive programs, structured enrichment (SE) attempts to impart knowledge in a linear and gradual fashion to improve the interpersonal dimensions of a marriage (L'Abate, 1985). At the base of SE is the belief that enrichment can help more couples than therapy. Thus, prevention, growth, and skill building are the various goals of SE.

Frederic E. Stevens, MA, of Atlanta GA, is currently with March for Peace.
Luciano L'Abate, PhD, is a Professor of Psychology, Georgia State University, Atlanta, GA 30303. Requests for reprints should be sent to the second author.

## Goals of Structured Enrichment

The aim of SE is to provide a way in which couples can join with one another to increase and to improve their interaction through novel face-to-face experiences. These experiences hopefully teach them alternative ways of relating to one another. These alternatives are administered in a standardized directly structured manner, such as teaching individual couples communication skills. In spite of the structured nature of SE, where trainers follow *verbatim* instructions through manuals, it provides space for couples to be both interactive and disclosing (L'Abate, 1985).

## SE and Other Enrichment Programs

What distinguishes SE from other forms of enrichment is the wide variety of programs which are designed to be administered around selected relationship issues. The three manuals (L'Abate & associates, 1975a; L'Abate & associates, 1975b; L'Abate & Slone, 1981) contain a total of 71 different programs. With this wide range of choices an enrichment program may be custom-tailored to suit the interpersonal needs of a particular couple. By moving flexibly around specific relationship issues, SE is able to confront a wide spectrum of marital issues. For instance, following are examples of the most commonly used programs.

1. Confronting change
2. Sexual clarification and fulfillment
3. Cohabitation
4. Reciprocity
5. Communication
6. Assertiveness
7. Working through
8. Conflict resolution

## The Process of SE

A standard SE program consists of six lessons requiring eight one-hour sessions which may take four to nine weeks to complete. The sessions follow a standard sequence of intake-pretest, six enrichment sessions, post-test, feedback and phone or questionnaire follow-up. The SE process begins with the initial intake interview to gain rapport with the couple. This rapport is gained through a simple questioning about how the couple met, etc. Also, at this point a couple is informed of what enrichment is about and what they may expect from it. A consent form is then signed which acts as a contract for enrichment.

With non-clinical, highly functioning couples, rapport is usually easily established. However, with some couples this initial interview may be indicative of future resistance to the enrichment process or the inappropriateness of enrichment. While some shyness and recalcitrance on the part of the couple is to be expected, continued ambivalence to gentle questioning about the marriage can be indicative of some underlying difficulties in the relationship. These difficulties may best be diagnosed in the second step of enrichment, the use of paper-and-pencil measures. Paper and pencil evaluation tools have included, in different combinations, a Family Information Sheet, Feelings About the Family Scale, a Marital Questionnaire, a Semantic Differential Sheet, the Azrin Marital Happiness Scale, the Spanier Dyadic Adjustment Scale, the Holmes-Rahe Schedule of Events, and the Family Adjustment Inventory (L'Abate & McHenry, 1983; L'Abate & Rupp, 1981).

The interview and paper and pencil evaluations serve as a way of tailor-making a specific course of SE as well as a measure of therapeutic change. This measurement is difficult to obtain since most couples are non-clinical and their scores may be above the norm in the pretest, which does not leave much room in the test scores for measureable positive change. However, the measures also serve a diagnostic function by pinpointing specific relationship issues to follow-up during SE.

From the subjective interview and the objective evaluation, a plan is made to offer to the couple a choice of three SE programs. Sometimes a couple will request attention in a particular interpersonal area. Most often, a couple is rather vague in specifying exactly why they want enrichment and what they want from it. In these instances, reliance on specific evaluation tools may indicate the specific area of enrichment for the couple.

In some cases, an individual will respond to a question about why they want enrichment by talking about what the spouse or partner needs to do. This individual may fault the partner or at least give some indications that it is the partner who needs enrichment. These situations plus poor scores on the various paper and pencil tests may be indicative of resistance on the part of at least one member and may suggest that the couple is at risk. Under these conditions, the enricher needs to explore whether the couple may need therapy rather than enrichment. Other indicators of a need for referral to therapy are far less subtle: (a) partners who seek enrichment when they are presently considering whether to end their relationship; (b) incidents of abuse, infidelity, and serious drug abuse are among the indicators of the need for more intensive interventions.

In the first enrichment session, the three possible programs are presented. There are few limits to the programs available to the couple.

If necessary, one may be designed for them. Following the selection of a program by the couple, the first session of SE begins as the enricher reads to the couple the sections that deal with the stated interests of the couple and the impression of the trainer from an SE manual.

During the course of SE, a program may be changed at any time. In some cases, a change will be planned contingent on the level of a couple's participation, or the level at which they perform in particular enrichment exercises. A couple may also request a change in the program saying the current one is too serious or does not suit them well.

Following the six enrichment sessions, a post-test feedback session is scheduled. The feedback seeks to discover the couple's impression of both the enricher and enrichment program. Then, the enricher shares his/her impressions with the couple. Invariably, these impressions are framed in a positive manner. Following this feedback, recommendations are made about whether they should continue to get more SE, be referred for therapeutic treatment, or nothing. Three months after the feedback, a follow-up questionnaire is sent to the couple.

## CASE STUDY: BILL AND SUSAN

This case was chosen for a number of reasons. First, it provides a look at the use of enrichment with a couple who seemed clinically at risk. Second, this case is illustrative of both the content and process of SE. Third, use of the programs with this couple demonstrates the flexibility which may be achieved with SE in the hands of someone knowledgeable in its application. Finally, this case hopes to capture the flavor of what actually occurs during SE.

### Pre-Interview and Pretest Assessment

Bill, aged 24, is an Army veteran. Born and reared in a small South Carolina town, he works in a job which takes him out of town for days at a time. He presented a relaxed, confident appearance.

Susan, aged 24, met Bill while they were both in the Army. She had lived "all over the country" but has not lived anywhere for more than a few years. She also works but does not have to leave town. She presented a rather reserved, thoughtful appearance.

### Pretest Assessment

The GSU Couples Battery included the following instruments: Concerning My Family, Feelings Questionnaire, Family Adjustment Scale, Dyadic Adjustment Scale, and the Holmes-Rahe Schedule of Events.

On the Feelings Questionnaire, Susan said Bill's relationship with her family was quite negative. Susan's difficulty with her parents may only have been projected onto Bill.

On the Dyadic Adjustment Scale, both of them checked that they were "happy" with their relationship. Both checked that they occasionally quarrel and that one of them left the house following a quarrel. Bill reported that he had at one time regretted being married and that they frequently disagreed on demonstrations of affection.

The Family Adjustment Scale (FAS) provides space for a couple to write in their own words areas of satisfaction and dissatisfaction. Susan chose to express her dissatisfactions more than Bill. On 9 of 10 specific behaviors, she made self-critical remarks. Of top priority she wrote, "Life . . . generally an observer rather than a participant." She listed her relationship with Bill, with others, and her personal development in negative ratios. On the other hand, Bill ranked Susan as "someone to confide in" (#2) and as "someone to love" (#1).

The FAS suggested that Susan rated high on low self-esteem. In addition, Susan appeared to have some difficulty accepting support. On the other hand, Bill may have offered support to Susan in an ineffective manner. This suggestion about Bill appeared supported in his style of answering on the FAS. He spoke in global terms, which were open to misinterpretation by those reading him, especially someone such as Susan. Susan allowed Bill to make important family decisions, including ones that she should make for herself. Thus, they both agreed to an imbalance of decision making, suggesting inadequate role differentiation and individuation in the marriage.

### Discussion

A number of areas appeared open for enrichment. The pretests and interview indicated that Bill and Susan quarrel, and on at least one occasion, conflict was resolved by one of them leaving the house. Bill leaves town frequently (often about once a week for three to four days), suggesting that this "natural" form of conflict resolution may have been used more often than either was consciously aware of. The imbalance in decision making suggested unclear role differentiation. Both agreed to these conclusions. If one attempts to balance this process, he/she may experience resistance from the other. Their affection for each other was unclearly expressed.

This couple had been married three years. Test results suggested that their relationship was barely functional. Trouble areas such as conflict resolution, role differentiation, and affective expression needed to be addressed.

From the intake interview and tests, the following SE programs were suggested: (1) Confronting Change (may be effective to overcome expected resistance); (2) Assertiveness (may help to rebalance the differentiation of marital roles); and (3) Communication (the most gentle of the programs that addresses conflict resolution, consequently, it may be more acceptable and may be usable despite its family orientation).

### First Session

After introduction of the three programs, Susan chose the program of Communication and Bill concurred. This program is designed for families but is adaptable for couples.

*Lesson 1: Unfair Communication.* This lesson revealed a number of communication practices that were blocking the couples' closeness. Susan confided that she used guilt when she felt that her needs were not being met. She would tell Bill when a need was not met and then "*lay on the guilt*" when he complained that task performances were not meeting his expectations. Bill's use of expectation appeared throughout the session. Clearly, this program had something to offer them. They both played the "numbers game" (i.e., they kept a score of wrongs inflicted by their partner). In addition, Bill reported that he used the silent treatment as a way to instill guilt in Susan. Also, when he saw an argument coming or when involved in an argument, he would "clam up." He clammed up to protect the marriage, to squelch an unhappy scene, and to escape an issue he did not want to have brought up again. He maintained that the arguments were usually soon forgotten.

What was evident from this lesson was that Bill and Susan had bountiful insights into their marriage. In this instance, the insight was being used to sustain the dysfunctional dimensions of their marriage. Despite the intellectual awareness of their transactions, no effort was made for changes. Bill's use of the silent treatment served to keep the relationship grounded by keeping Susan confused about what was going on in the relationship. In effect, he was saying, "I am unsatisfied with your dissatisfactions about my showing a lack of affection for your not doing as much for us as I am. To dramatize my point, I will not talk about my dissatisfactions." Bill had the added impetus of being able to leave her and go out of town for three to five days at a time during an average week. These departures could not be avoided, but they did not help the marriage. In view of this sequence of events, it was no wonder that he experienced the arguments as forgotten. The lesson ended with a home work assignment.

*Lesson 2: Hurtful Communication.* This lesson begins to deal with disagreements and how they are resolved. Following some resistance, Bill and Susan settled into one of their common issues, Bill's lack of expressing affection. When asked about nagging, Susan reeled off a list of her most common naggings. Each issue focused on intimacy and affection. She complained that Bill was often too busy to be affectionate. He replied that when he had been affectionate, she was cold and unresponsive. This clear disparity had gone unresolved despite apparent good intentions.

It became apparent that fear of fighting coupled with a fear of closeness kept this couple in a constant state of stand-off. The intellectualization of insight was used to maintain the imbalance of the marriage.

*Lesson 3: Negotiation.* Bill and Susan were found to experience more conflict than was previously thought to occur. Consequently, the program was changed from Communication to Negotiation. Negotiation was chosen because it focuses on the use of silent treatment as a form of communication. In addition, the entire program goes into conflict resolution in a more in-depth manner. The couple agreed to the change.

Two lessons (Communication and Hurt) were completed in the same session. Throughout this session a thread of enmeshment became clearer. Bill responded, not to Susan, but at how she fulfilled his expectations of her. Each was afraid of what the other was feeling. Each was afraid to let the other know how he/she was feeling. Afraid to self-disclose, they were unable to get close. In a later exercise, Bill consistently changed statements that were supposed to begin with "I" (self-disclosure) to statements beginning with "I think that you . . . " In addition, Susan played victim in this dialogue. Bill rescued her by preaching to her on one level and blaming on another level. Thus, Bill kept from having to self-disclose.

*Lesson 4.* Susan reported that when Bill yelled at her, she feared physical violence would occur. She qualified this report by adding that there had been no physical violence. She often tried to second-guess what Bill was thinking and would interrupt what he was trying to convey to her. In short, she tried to do his thinking for him, which was seen as a fear of knowing his real thoughts and an inability to accept their differences. Bill regarded this second-guessing as an invasion of his privacy.

*Lesson 5: Trust.* Two lessons were also done in one session. Bill and Susan reported having resolved an argument using "I" statements. They did not list their hurts as requested in one exercise. Both were apparently resistant to the exercises of this lesson, occasionally saying that the exercises were irrelevant to them and their marriage. Both claimed that they had a very honest, trusting relationship and that there was little they feared or hid from each other. Susan thought the first exercise was attempting to "open a can of worms" and then withdrew the remark. Bill remained silent.

In the area of dishonesty, Bill said that he did not relate to Susan everything that he did when he went out of town. He used to, but she became so uncomfortable with it that he stopped. The issue went unresolved. Bill then displayed a recognition of himself that he wished to try out. He reported being afraid that feeling expressed to her may not be his real feelings. Because of this fear, he could not be intimate when he did not feel like it.

*Lesson 6: Quid Pro Quo.* As Bill summarized back to Susan what she wanted to see in him, he interrupted his own recall. He said in a defensive tone that what Susan wanted to see in him were all things directed toward meeting her needs. Susan recanted and said that the things she wants to see in him were things for him, not her. She said that he "completely misunderstood everything I said. I want you to relax and enjoy it for yourself. To do things for *you!*" Bill appeared unable to accept any sort of support.

On the other hand, Susan could voice her needs concretely and plainly. Despite this quality, Bill said that he could not fully understand her. She requested more direct, spontaneous, and verbal support. Bill concluded by saying that he wanted to return to good times together, like they used to have.

### Pre-Test and Post-Test Comparison

On the Dyadic Adjustment Scale, Susan made no significant changes. Her score remained about the same. Bill also showed few changes. On the Family Adjustment Scale, Susan ranked as #1 that she needs to be more dependable. This ranking reflected how Bill had conveyed to her that her dependability served to validate him. Bill ranked as #1 and #2 his dissatisfaction with his lack of emotional expression and his lack of spontaneity. He suggested, more than he had done previously, a more specific problem-solving approach to their communication. He assumed more personal ownership of the difficulties. Hopefully, this new-found awareness was more than intellectual insight! On the Feelings Questionnaire, both reported that they were "slightly negative" about how each understood the other. Once again, on this questionnaire as on all pre- and post-test measures, scores were quite high, suggestion that neither was willing to recognize their fusion and polarization. They do appear, however, to be slightly more aware of the problems.

The changes from pre- to post-test were not significant, although there was some movement in a positive direction from one test to another. Probably this marriage might have to get worse before it gets better.

### Feedback Session

Bill and Susan were told that their willingness to talk, as well as their trust and determination were greatly appreciated. They were cautioned that their determination might hamper them in efforts to resolve conflict.

The suggestion was made that each continue to take more ownership, as they had done in SE, of their difficulties by using more "I" statements and fewer "you" statements. They were told that their intellectual and verbal skills were of a high quality, but their intellectual awareness and insight without action are meaningless. Finally, they were told that their love for each other was very real and deep. As they really do love each other, they wanted to give the other their very best. In order to give their best, they would have to grow individually as persons and not as each other's mirror images. In short, to be really close, they must be separate.

A future plan was outlined for their marriage. Possible interventions were suggested. Susan, however, resented this suggestion. The door to the various forms of treatment was left open for them.

## CONCLUSION

SE provided an introduction to change and did not push them into what they were not ready for, i.e., therapeutic intervention that might be required in the future. In this way, the program may have served an effective outreach and preventative function.

Perhaps the major shortcoming of the entire program was its brevity. The couple was beginning to adopt new negotiation skills in the fifth session. Interestingly, a follow-up questionnaire indicated at least some maintenance of their gain.

## REFERENCES

Azrin, N. H., Master, B. H., & Jones, R. (1973). Reciprocity counseling: A rapid learning-based procedure for marital counseling. *Behavior Research and Therapy, 11*, 365–382.
L'Abate. (1985). Structured enrichment (SE) with couples and families. *Family Relations, 34*, 169–175.
L'Abate, L., & associates. (1975a). *Manual: Family enrichment programs*. Atlanta, GA: Social Research Laboratories.
L'Abate, L., & associates. (1975b). *Manual: Enrichment programs for the family life cycle*. Atlanta, GA: Social Research Laboratories.
L'Abate, L., & McHenry, S. (1983). *Handbook of marital interventions*. New York: Grune & Stratton.
L'Abate, L. & Rupp, G. (1981). *Enrichment: Skills training for family life*. Washington, DC: University Press.
L'Abate, L., & Sloan, S. Z. (Eds.). (1981). *Workbook for family enrichment: Development and structural dimensions*. Atlanta, GA: Georgia State University.
Mace, D. R. (Ed.). (1983). *Prevention in family services: Approaches to family wellness*. Beverly Hills, CA: Sage Publications.
Otto, H. A. (Ed.). (1976). *Marriage and family enrichment: New perspectives and programs*. Nashville, TN: Abingdon.
Satir, V. (1967). *Conjoint family therapy*. Palo Alto, CA: Science and Behavior Books.

# Starting a Local
# Marriage Enrichment Group

Wallace Denton

**ABSTRACT.** The central focus of this essay is the description of a model of marriage and family enrichment which can be utilized in communities where enrichment leaders are not available. The model calls for using a couple who may have limited experience with enrichment to serve as facilitators who help the group members discover their own resources. The format includes inviting only couples with basically strong marriages, the careful avoidance of advice giving, and the major portion of the time in each session being spent with just the husband-wife dyad in private discussion. The content relies heavily upon stimulus material designed to be used by enrichment groups.

Couples who participate in weekend types of marriage enrichment experiences commonly report feeling revitalized; they often report a renewed sense of intimacy and commitment in their marriages (Lester & Doherty, 1983; Mace & Mace, 1976). However, there is evidence that if nothing more is done, the enthusiasm, new resolve and behavioral changes initiated during any type of enrichment experience are gradually lost (Baum, 1978; Doherty, McCabe, Ryder, 1978; Guldner, 1971). For this reason, David and Vera Mace, pioneers in marriage enrichment, have urged that local groups of couples organize to meet regularly to preserve gains made in enrichment experiences as well as provide support for each other (Mace & Mace, 1976).

That some type of follow up is needed is understandable. Almost everything else needs preventive upkeep. Just as we do preventive maintenance on our auto, and have regular medical and dental checkups, even so do we need regular marital checkups. It may be that in marriage enrichment, the vehicle exists for developing preventive programs for marriages at the local community level.

The purpose of this essay is to describe a plan for developing ongoing local marriage enrichment groups, even in communities where trained enrichment leadership is not available. It is addressed to those members of the helping professions who recognize the value of enrichment, but

---

Wallace Denton, EdD, is Professor of Family Therapy in the Department of Child Development and Family Studies, Purdue University, West Lafayette, IN 47907.

who may not have either the time or training in enrichment to personally develop and lead such a group. The intent of the essay is to provide this professional with sufficient information that he or she can either develop and lead an enrichment group or else enlist the aid and supervise another person in leading a group.

## LOCATING A MARRIAGE ENRICHMENT GROUP

The professional who wants to refer a client couple to a marriage enrichment group often finds it frustrating to find one. Three reasons account for this first, the movement is new enough that relatively few communities have ongoing groups; secondly, marriage enrichment is a rather unorganized, grass-roots movement with no strong, central office promoting it; thirdly, the marriage enrichment programs that do exist are largely one-time weekend events with no follow up programs in the couples' home communities.

Nevertheless, if groups exist at the local levels, these can be identified by making inquiries of key community leaders in the helping professions. For instance, a priest in the local Roman Catholic Church may know how to contact persons involved in Marriage Encounter. Other clergy may know of other marriage enrichment possibilities. If there is a college in the city, inquiries in the department of psychology or sociology may turn up a marriage enrichment resource. Failing at that, a call or letter to the national office of ACME, Marriage Encounter, or one of the other groups listed in the ''Resources'' section of this collection will bring information as to where the nearest group is located.

In other situations it may be that the only available leadership lives some distance away. If this is the case, several couples can be recruited to participate in a weekend event and share the expense of the leaders' travel, lodging and honorarium. Reservations can be made at a retreat center, though this writer has led such groups where couples simply went across town to a local motel with meeting facilities. (Everyone stayed at the motel and sessions were held in a conference room.)

## DEVELOPING LOCAL LEADERSHIP

Perhaps the best way to get a group going at the local level is to begin with having all prospective members in a weekend retreat. Once the weekend retreat is concluded, the group can continue even without trained leadership by using leadership developed from within the group. In fact, what is being suggested is that someone like the reader consider organizing and leading such a group! (The reader obviously has some interest in marriage enrichment as evidenced by reading this. He or she also likely has relevant training in the behavioral sciences.) In an "expert" oriented society like ours, such a suggestion may come as a surprise. However, self-help groups have been around a long time. Alcoholics Anonymous and Parents Without Partners are two of the better known such groups led by people without the usual professional credentials. These groups usually provide a forum in which a person can think through his or her situation, set personal goals, and have the encouragement and support of friends who are in the same basic situation (alcoholic, solo parent, etc.). While those attending a marriage enrichment group typically have not "hit bottom" maritally (to use a term familiar to those in A. A.), the enrichment group does provide a forum in which the couple can examine their relationship, set goals, and have the support of the group who are also dealing with similar issues.

L'Abate (1981) observes that self-help groups have grown out of various skill-training programs, of which marriage enrichment is one expression. Guerney (1969) also found that persons with limited professional credentials can, with some training, serve as competent facilitators. Such individuals bring to the group interpersonal skills in facilitating interaction.

It is the belief of this author that what is needed in working with a marriage enrichment group is not leadership in the usual meaning of the word, where someone with expert knowledge attempts to transmit that knowledge to a lay audience. Rather, in marriage enrichment, what is needed are leaders who serve as *facilitators* (Mace & Mace, 1976; Otto, 1975). A facilitator is a person (a husband-wife team is strongly recommended) skilled in enabling the group to discover and develop their own resources. Even in cases where marriage enrichment leaders are professionally trained, they still serve as facilitators in aiding couples to interact with each other in such a way that they can discover their own answers to a more rewarding relationship. However, nothing said here is to depreciate competent, trained leadership for marriage enrichment programs. Rather, the present approach is designed for the many communities where trained leadership is not available, but couples still want to do something about their marriages.

What of the possible problems or hurt caused by someone with little or no training? This, of course, needs to be addressed. Negative things can certainly happen. However, if the guidelines set forth in the program outlined herein are followed, the possibility of negative effects will be reduced. One safeguard involves the fact that only couples with basically strong marriages are invited into the group. Concerns of doing damage to couples with basically healthy marriages is slender. Also, the giving of advice is strictly forbidden. Beyond this, after spending over twenty-five years working as a family therapist with clinical populations, this writer is less concerned about having some negative impact on the family than about having *any* impact at all! Homeostatic forces in most families are strong enough that the possibility of serious damage is minimized.

## THE PARTICIPANT SELECTION PROCESS

A major issue in any venture as this has to do with the selection of participants. Unfortunately, virtually no research has been done on the type of couples which make the best candidates for marriage enrichment. However, a related surprise finding of Giblin, Sprenkle and Sheehan's (1985) meta-analysis of the enrichment research literature was that couples with a greater magnitude of conflict seemed to benefit most from enrichment. Still, research into the types of couples which can and cannot benefit from enrichment needs to be done.

However, for the model being proposed here, one in which the facilitators are lay persons, the following guidelines are proposed for making participant selection:

1. Only invite couples who seem to have reasonably healthy and growing marriages. The experience of the author in leading marriage enrichment groups is that couples with severe conflicts often find the program to activate marital wounds in such a way that the whole group suffers. As Otto (1975) observes, enrichment is for couples who have "well-functioning marriages." One cannot enrich that which does not already have richness.

This raises the question as to how one decides whether a couple has a basically sound marriage? Of course, there is no fail-proof method. However, most observant and sensitive people are able to sense something about the stresses and quality of their close friends' marriages. This is an argument for inviting people whom the organizers know, and to invite those with whom they feel comfortable. People are not likely to be open with those who leave them feeling uncomfortable.

2. Invite five to seven couples to be a part of the enrichment group. A larger group than this tends to become a crowd and is counterproductive to discussion and a willingness to be open. Furthermore, it is suggested that the group meet in members' homes, and a larger group often cannot be comfortably accommodated in most homes.

3. Invite no one into the group who seems to dominate a discussion or has strong needs to give advice or otherwise control groups in which they find themselves. This is a further argument for inviting only people known well to the organizers. Some people seem to see themselves as "natural born" counselors. They compulsively give advice by beginning sentences with, "If I were you . . . " The format of this model allows *no giving of advice to other couples by anyone in the group.*

4. Avoid couples where one or both seem to be overly dependent and thereby "invite" others to give advice or otherwise rescue them from themselves. These people will dominate the group in a backhanded way by subtly luring group members into focusing on the dependent person's problems.

## ENRICHMENT GROUP "GROUND RULES"

Having selected the group, it is important at the first session to orient the members to the format to be followed. This is particularly true for couples who may have never been a part of a marriage enrichment program. Without the orientation, they will follow the only models to which they have been exposed, which probably involved lectures and passive listening. Some may expect it to be a "fun and games" program. Even if couples have been part of another marriage enrichment program, the present model is somewhat different.

These "ground rules" seem important to group functioning;

1. Regular attendance is important. Couples who attend irregularly have trouble being integrated into the group and thereby have difficulty becoming caring and supportive members. Moreover, individuals who cannot attend a session should be encouraged to notify the facilitators if they will be absent. Otherwise, groups sometimes delay starting by thinking a particular couple is running late.

2. Members are to attend as couples. Marriage enrichment with only one person present is almost a contradiction of terms. The program will be rather meaningless if a person attempts to come by him or herself.

3. Indicate that there will be no lectures and that most of the time will be spent alone as a couple discussing the relevance of the sessions' topic for themselves. In fact, the most important part of the session will be their private discussions together.

4. There will be an opportunity following the private discussion time for group discussion. However, it should be made clear that no one *has* to say or share anything which makes him or her uncomfortable. Members may have heard of groups where everyone is pressured into sharing deeply personal matters. Reassurance needs to be given that this is not that type of group. However, it is hoped that there will be some sharing of experience around the topic of discussion. If no one says anything, everybody can have a cup of coffee and go home!

At this point it should be noted that this is quite different from the typical marriage enrichment group which has trained leadership. While openness is possible in the model proposed here, leaders with little training ought not try to probe too deeply during discussion time. Nonetheless, the facilitators can model open discussion by sharing something from their own relationship and thereby encourage other couples to share.

5. No advice will be given by anyone in the group to other participants. Instead, it is quite acceptable to share what one's experience has been with the topic under discussion. Indications of advice giving usually being with, "I think you should . . . " or "If I were you I would . . . " or something similar. Ideally, permission should be given by all participants for others to be alert for advice giving so that the speaker can be asked to restate what is being said into what his or her experience has been with the subject. Among friends, advice giving is a good way to put stress on the friendship. Of course, even in groups with trained leadership, advice giving is usually inappropriate and seldom given.

## MARRIAGE ENRICHMENT PROGRAM FORMAT

The program format of this model is rather simple. It is as follows:

1. The group agrees upon the time, place, and frequency of sessions. This is done at the first session. The group might, for example, consider agreeing to meet for six months and then reassess whether to continue. The experience of the author is that meeting in a home once a month for about an hour and a half seems to be optimal. Meeting longer and more frequently seems to contribute to boredom and burn-out with the group. The host home can provide coffee and desert, unless other arrangements are made. The meeting can be rotated among couples whose homes are large enough to accommodate the group. Meeting in homes seems to provide a warm and informal atmosphere which is conducive to developing a sense of closeness among group members.

Quitting on time is important since some couples have to get home to relieve the baby sitter. However, couples may choose to linger after the formal meeting is over, but that is their choice.

2. Use materials from a book, tape, or other source to provide the content basis for the focus of each session. Several books are on the market which have been written for use with marriage enrichment groups. For instance, *Creative Couples: The Growth Factor in Marriage* written by the author and his wife (Denton & Denton, 1983) was written with small enrichment groups specifically in mind. This book, as with some other books, also has questions and exercises to go with each chapter to help stimulate discussion. A different chapter can be assigned for reading in connection with each session. Two additional books are recommended for use with marriage enrichment groups: Howard and Charlotte Clinebell (1970), *The Intimate Marriage*, and Robert and Carrie Dale (1978), *Making Good Marriages Better*. Each of these books was written with marriage enrichment groups in mind. Questions and exercises accompa-

nying each chapter make them especially useful for the model of enrichment being described here.

3. A facilitator begins each session by briefly summarizing the assigned chapter. (This task can also be assigned to another group member.) No speech or lecture is necessary, or appropriate. Some discussion may emerge at this point which helps couples begin thinking about the topic. Sometimes a worksheet or questions from the book can be reproduced and passed out to help guide the individual couples in their dialogue with each other. By taking this approach, facilitators with limited backgrounds in working with enrichment groups are spared feeling that they must develop a lecture on some facet of family relations. The book provides the basic structure for this purpose. In any case, within 5–15 minutes (depending on how much discussion takes place at this stage, the group moves to the next phase.

4. Couples are then assigned to different rooms in the house by the host or hostess to privately discuss as a couple the relevance of the session's topic for themselves. The author's experience has been that 40–45 minutes seems to be adequate time for this part of the program. When couples are finished, they begin collecting back in the meeting room, have a cup of coffee and chat until the whole group has reassembled.

5. Group discussion takes place following the time of dyadic interaction. After the group recollects, a facilitator can ask, "Did anyone learn anything which you care to share?" Don't be surprised if no one rushes in to speak. The facilitator couple might be prepared to lead off by sharing something. Most of the time this is sufficient to get others talking. As is probably apparent, the facilitators are also participants and talk together during the private time along with other couples. Other leading questions are: "Did anyone make any decisions which you care to share?" or "Were you surprised by anything you said or did?" or "What did you do or say that made you pleased with yourself?"

When time for the meeting is over, the chapter or assignment for the next session is made, and everyone has another cup of coffee and goes home.

## Limitations of This Model

As is apparent, this model of marriage enrichment will not work well with all populations and situations. It appears to work best with those people who have some ability for introspection and a willingness to verbally interact with the mate in a nondefensive manner. It assumes participants have an ability to be self-directing and self-motivated since there is no trained leader to help bring these factors into focus. Of course, this model would be handicapped by group members who attempt to work out their own interpersonal problems by heavy advice giving and otherwise "straightening out" other members. Such behavior would have a negative impact on any group, but in this case the absence of trained leaders who know how to curb such members might lead to a slow disintegration of the group.

## SUMMARY

This article has briefly described approaches to starting a local marriage enrichment group with emphasis on an approach to marriage enrichment that employs a leader couple with limited background in marriage enrichment. This approach is designed for those hundreds of communities across the nation where no one with training is readily available to lead such groups. The content for discussions is provided by using books or other stimulus materials designed for marriage enrichment groups. The group is structured so that no one gives advice, which minimizes the possibility of negative effects which might otherwise come from such groups. Central to this model's approach is the spending of a major portion of the time with each husband-wife dyad engaged in a private discussion about the relevance of the topic of the day for their lives. This creates a private forum in which the two can talk, plan, negotiate about some aspects of their marriage. In that sense, it is little different from what they might do were they to discuss the topic at home. However, by meeting as a group with other couples, this puts some necessity upon them to engage in a dialogue with each other and also provides time for group discussion.

By following this format, it is possible for groups of couples to get together much like other self-help groups and bring support and direction to their marriages by aiding them in tapping into their own resources for growth and enrichment.

## REFERENCES

Bader, E., Microys, G., Sinclair, C., Willet, E., Conway, B. (1980). Do marriage preparation programs really work?: A Canadian Experiment. *Journal of Marital and Family Therapy*, 6(2), 171–179.

Baum, M.C. (1978). The short-term, long-term, and differential effects of group versus bibliotherapy relationship enhancement program for couples (Doctoral dissertation, University of Texas at Austin, 1977). *Dissertation Abstracts International*, 38, 6132B-6133B.

Clinebell, H. & Clinebell, C. (1970). *The Intimate Marriage*. New York: Harper and Row.

Dale, R. & Dale, C. (1978). *Making Good Marriages Better*. Nashville: Broadman Press.

Denton, W. & Denton, J. (1983). *Creative Couples: The Growth Factor in Marriage*. Philadelphia: Westminster Press.

Doherty, W.J., McCable, P. & Ryder, R.G. (1978). Marriage encounter: A critical appraisal. *Journal of Marriage and Family Counseling*, 4(4), 99–107.

Giblin, P., Sprenkle, D.D. & Sheehan, R. (1985). Enrichment outcome research: A meta-analysis of premarital, marital, and family findings. *Journal of Marital and Family Therapy, 11*(3).

Guerney, B.G. (Ed.). (1969). *Psychotherapeutic Agents: New Roles for Non-Professionals, Parents & Teachers.* New York: Holt.

Guldner, C.A. (1971). The post-marital: An alternative to premarital counseling. *Family Coordinator, 20,* 115–119.

L'Abate, L. (1981). Skill training programs for couples and families. In A.S. Gurman and D.P. Kniskern (Eds.), *Handbook of Family Therapy* (pp. 631–661). New York: Brunner/Mazel.

Lester, M.E. & Doherty, W.J. (1983). Couples' long-term evaluations of their marriage encounter weekend. *Journal of Marital and Family Therapy, 9*(2), 183–188.

Mace, D. & Mace, V. (1976). Marriage enrichment: A preventive group approach to couples. In David H.L. Olson (Ed.), *Treating Relationships* (pp. 321–336). Lake Mills, IA: Graphic Publishing Co.

Otto, H. (1975). Marriage and family enrichment programs in North America—Report and analysis. *The Family Coordinator, 24*(2), 137–142.

# Research and Assessment in Marriage and Family Enrichment: A Meta-Analysis Study

## Paul Giblin

**ABSTRACT.** This study sought to integrate and evaluate existing enrichment research literature, most of which had never been published. Meta-analysis, the review technique used in the study, is a new method for statistically aggregating and evaluating empirical findings. Eighty-five studies of premarital, marital and family enrichment, representing 3,886 couples or families were gathered and their results statistically aggregated. Findings from the study are discussed in terms of overall enrichment effectiveness as well as salient program, subject, design and measurement characteristics. Implications of these findings are discussed.

Since the early 1970's there has been a rapid growth of structured, experiential programs designed to enhance marriages and families. Enrichment programs with national stature include Marriage Encounter, Relationship Enhancement, Couple Communication Program, Association of Couples for Marriage Enrichment (ACME), and for families, Family Cluster and Understanding Us. Such programs generally seek (1) to increase self-awareness and awareness of partners, especially regarding strengths and growth potentials of the individuals and the relationship; (2) to increase exploration and self-disclosure of feelings and thoughts; (3) to increase mutual empathy and intimacy; and (4) to develop and encourage the use of skills needed for effective communication, problem-solving and conflict resolution (Hof & Miller, 1981). Further, enrichment programs serve (1) to provide a sense of belonging and community for couples and families (Sawin, 1979), and (2) to facilitate the role-making, role-taking process characteristic of marriage today (Miller, Nunnally & Wackman, 1979).

Considerable research has been conducted on various enrichment programs (Brock & Joanning, 1983; Guerney, 1977; Milholland & Avery, 1982) and specific programmatic, subject, and measurement characteristics (Hof, Epstein, & Miller, 1980; L'Abate, 1981; Wampler, 1982). Previous reviews of enrichment research have yielded generally

---

Paul Giblin, PhD, is Supervisor of New Hampshire Catholic Charities, Rochester, NH 03867.

positive assessments of treatment effectiveness (Gurman & Kniskern, 1977; Hof & Miller, 1981). However, the need to integrate and assess this rapidly expanding, and at times conflicting body of research literature in a quantitative fashion is paramount. The present review investigated the effectiveness of enrichment programs through the use of such a quantitative approach, meta-analysis.

Glass (1976) defined meta-analysis as the statistical analysis of a large collection on analytic results from individual studies for the purpose of integrating these findings. A meta-analysis is conducted on a group of studies with common conceptual hypotheses or common operational definitions of independent or dependent variables. Study findings are transformed to common expressions of treatment effectiveness, i.e., effect sizes. Features of studies that might influence findings are defined, measured, and their covariation controlled or examined. The summary statistic of meta-analysis has the range and distribution of a Z-score statistic. A positive effect size indicates that the treated group improved more than the untreated group; a negative effect size indicates that the untreated group improves more than the treated group. The larger the effect size, the greater the magnitude of effect. In areas like developmental, social, personality, and clinical research, relatively small effects are the norm; typically the range from $-1$ to $+1$ (Landman & Dawes, 1982).

Meta-analysis is especially relevant to the enrichment area;

1. While considerable research has been conducted on enrichment programs, these findings are largely unpublished, and thus research has not tended to build on previous research (Wampler, 1982). The current study aggregated and evaluated these findings.
2. Enrichment is generally limited to "normal and healthy" couples and families. Treatment-induced change for this population will likely tend to be less dramatic than for a clinic population. Assessment therefore needs to be able to attend to small changes. A meta-analytic review provides a more quantitative assessment of outcome than previous review forms and hence, is more responsive to small treatment effects.
3. Meta-analysis serves the dual purpose of generating and testing hypotheses. The description of treatment characteristics associated with outcome is especially relevant to a relatively new field like enrichment.

A major limitation of meta-analysis must be noted at the outset. It is a post hoc procedure. While hypotheses may be stated in advance of data collection, successful hypothesis testing is entirely depending upon the existence of adequate numbers and ranges of studies and outcome measures. A meta-analysis researcher does not conduct any additional studies, but rather reviews and extracts information from existing studies and then makes judgments as to the adequacy of the resultant population (or sample) of effect sizes. As a result of this limitation, meta-analysis in areas that are largely underdeveloped most typically focus on main effects. This limitation was present, more often than not, in the present research.

## METHOD

The reader is referred to Giblin, Sprenkle and Sheehan (1985) for detailed explanation of the methodology employed in the present research, for further discussion of findings, and for an evaluation of meta-analysis as it applies to the family area. The interested reader is further referred to the special issue, February 1983, of the *Journal of Consulting and Clinical Psychology* for extensive discussion of the strengths and limitations of this methodology.

## RESULTS AND DISCUSSION

Following an extensive literature search, 85 studies were considered appropriate for inclusion in the meta-analysis. The resultant data pool included 3,886 couples or families from a variety of age, income, education levels and geographic areas. This data base generated 1,691 effect sizes.

The enrichment studies included in the present research yielded an average effect size of .44. Based on Choen (1977) and Tallmadge (1977), effect sizes were interpreted as follows: an effect size of .33 or less was considered small; from .34 to .66 was considered moderate; from .67 and up was considered large. Therefore, based on the 85 studies included in this meta-analysis, the conclusion is drawn that enrichment does indeed work. By contrast, Smith, Glass and Miller (1980) found that psychotherapy has an effect size of .85. Therefore, while not as powerful as psychotherapy, enrichment interventions are effective.

A danger of meta-analysis is placing undue emphasis on the single summary effect size. The primary asset of meta-analysis is the ability to examine those factors thought to influence outcome. Hence, effect size averages were examined according to five clusters of variables: source characteristics, program characteristics, subject characteristics, research design used in studies, and measurement characteristics of studies.

*Source*

Studies spanned the period 1971 to 1982. Seventy-five percent ($n =$ 64) of the studies were unpublished dissertations or manuscripts. No significant differences were observed based on date of study. This finding was disappointing as one would expect that enrichment research would become more refined over time. A common finding in meta-analytic reviews is significantly higher effects associated with published literature. The present study proved no exception; significantly higher effects were associated with journal articles and book chapters than with unpublished dissertations. This finding underlines the observation that one's sampling strategy can clearly influence outcome (Strube & Hartman, 1983). That is, a literature review based on published findings only, likely overestimates effect sizes.

*Program*

Significant variations were found across the three enrichment areas, premarital, marital and family and 23 program types. Combined effect size averages for the three areas were premarital, .526 ($n = 43$); marital, .419 ($n = 657$); and family, .545 ($n = 121$).

*Premarital.* Twelve studies examined the effectiveness of premarital preparation programs. Two studies require special mention. Bader and colleagues (1980) utilized the concept of a post-wedding component to premarital programming, with outcome measured at six and twelve months post-wedding. Bader's findings indicated that treatment couples steadily and significantly increased their conflict resolution skills, and more so from the six-month to one year interview than from the premarriage to six-month interview. This finding suggests that post-wedding sessions provide an effective complement to premarital preparations, and lends support to those calling for preventive approaches during the first year of marriage (Mace, 1984).

Miller (1971) assessed the effectiveness of a premarital communications program, noting that couples demonstrating greatest gains in a work style of communicating were (a) those couples closest to marriage and (b) couples with both partners having a stated purpose for joining the program. A point made by the above two studies and others (Schumm & Denton, 1979) is that premarital assessment needs to incorporate extended time frames of at least one year.

*Marital.* The most heavily researched marital programs were Couple Communication Program, Relationship Enhancement and Marriage Encounter. Noticeably absent were research studies on ACME (Association of Couples for Marriage Enrichment) programs. The only enrichment program with effect size averages in the large range was Guerney's

Relationship Enhancement program (ES = .96). This enrichment program, which seeks to teach communication skills of good sending and listening, and which lasts for 18 to 20 hours, far outdistanced Couple Communication Program (ES = .44) and Marriage Encounter (ES = .42). Additional work is now needed comparing these three programs across specific skill and attitudinal areas, with healthy and clinic populations, and with attention to durability of specific effects across time.

*Family.* Thirteen family enrichment studies were evaluated. Noticeably absent were studies of Sawin's Family Cluster program. Only two studies evaluated Carnes' Understanding Us Program. Guerney's Parent Adolescent Relationship Development program was again associated with the largest effect size average (ES = .96). Understanding Us, a program designed to enhance family cohesion and satisfaction as well as understanding ("not a methods course, not intended to teach a special set of skills", Carnes, 1981), had an effect size average of .27.

A factor examined within family studies was whether or not whole families were encouraged to attend, with whole family attendance hypothesized to be associated with larger effect sizes. In fact, significantly larger effect sizes were associated with the parent-child dyad or the couple dyad than with whole families ($F = 21.05$, $p = <.001$). Collett (1979) and Sprenkle (1980), using the same sample, reported a trend favoring couple only versus whole family on measures of satisfaction, communications and self-concept. Stanley (1980) compared parents only versus parents and adolescents, observing that the former group changed more on attitudinal measures, while the latter group showed more behavior change, more follow-through with continued family meetings, and greater change in adolescent decision-making.

Comparison of whole family versus specific subsets requires further examination. Within the present study, for example, a significant interaction may explain the dyad preference in outcome. That is, parent-adolescent programs most frequently involved more distressed subjects, taught communication skills, and assessed on mainly behavior measures; the variables diagnosis, outcome area, and type of measure were all individually associated with significantly greater outcome.

Across all types of programs the lowest effect sizes were found for attention placebo and discussion groups. Such groups seek to parallel treatment on factors such as number and length of sessions, type and quality of leadership, and leader attention; they diverge from treatment by emphasizing insight and excluding behavioral practice of skills. The present findings appear to indicate two important things: (a) Little change can be expected across outcome measures when primary program emphasis is on insight and understanding only with no attention to behavioral rehearsal; (b) time spent together may be a necessary but insufficient factor

Table 1

Effect Sizes for Specific Programs

| Program | ES | s | N |
|---|---|---|---|
| Premarital | .526 | .788 | 43 |
| Marital | .419 | .583 | 657 |
| Couple Comm Prog | .437 | .488 | 124 |
| Modified CCP | .301 | .636 | 32 |
| Relat Enhanc | .963 | .881 | 54 |
| Modified RE | .413 | .371 | 26 |
| Marriage Encntr | .416 | .693 | 59 |
| Modified ME | .381 | .316 | 27 |
| Religious Prog | .386 | .581 | 16 |
| Discuss-att plac | .219 | .552 | 60 |
| Comm training | .394 | .600 | 78 |
| Behavior Exch | .212 | .432 | 66 |
| Comb comm-behav | .445 | .338 | 21 |
| Choice Awareness | .387 | .424 | 29 |
| Rational Emot | .042 | .369 | 10 |
| Recip Cnsling | .363 | .564 | 3 |
| Pairing Enrich | .363 | .286 | 12 |
| Other | .583 | .474 | 40 |
| Family | .545 | .812 | 121 |
| Understnd Us | .266 | .417 | 13 |
| Par Ad Rel Dev | .961 | .723 | 37 |
| Communications | .633 | .959 | 41 |
| Discuss-att plac | .007 | .396 | 26 |
| Other | .195 | .762 | 4 |

for change. This finding is consistent with observations of several premarital program evaluations concerning the ineffectiveness, if not harm, of traditional lecture formats (Bader et al., 1980; Olson, 1983).

Several program characteristics were examined relative to effect size. Program length was found to significantly influence outcome; no differences were observed for program structure, cost, leader experience level, specificity of goals, or program format.

Programs ranged widely in length, from 2 to 36 hours, with the average program lasting 14 hours. The Pearson Correlation for program length with effect size was .156, $p = .001$, indicating a small positive relationship between length of program and effect size.

Programs were coded as to degree of structure for both leaders and participants. Programs overall rated moderately to highly structured, with higher structured programs having a significant but probably meaningless ($<.10$) correlation with effect size. Absent from the data pool were Mace's ACME program and Sawin's Family Cluster, both of which have less structure and emerging or evolving designs; such programs appear not to have been studied in controlled conditions.

Hypotheses were stated in advance that programs of greater cost, greater experience level of leadership, greater specificity of program goals and a format that combined weekend intensity with weekly practice would be associated with larger effect sizes. These hypotheses were not confirmed. Eighty-five percent of effect sizes fell into either weekend ($n$ = 84) or weekly ($n$ = 585) format, with no significant differences observed between formats. Two studies directly compared the weekend and weekly formats: Dorlac (1981) reported no significant differences on measures of intimacy and communication; Davis (1982) reported more positive gains for couples in a weekly program on measures of marital adjustment.

Diverse combinations of persons lead enrichment programs, i.e., married couples, unrelated male and female teams, individual males. No one category emerged as dominant. However, if all categories of two or more persons are combined, then co-leadership emerges as the form of choice. Leadership was also coded for experience level, with no significant differences observed. One study directly compared leader experience levels on outcome and reported a trend favoring graduate student marriage and family therapists over experienced or novice paraprofessionals (Roberts, 1974).

## Subject

A variety of questions were examined concerning who makes up the enrichment population and who appears to benefit most and least from enrichment interventions. Ten subject characteristics were examined. These characteristics were based on a data pool of 3,886 couples or families and included a total of 8,365 individuals. Subject education level and diagnosis were found to be significantly related to outcome, while age, income, years of marriage, gender, religion, life stage and previous enrichment experience showed no significant relationship with outcome.

Ages of participants ranged from 18 to 43 years ($\overline{X}$ = 32 years). Education levels ranged from 11 to 17 years ($\overline{X}$ = 15 years). Enrichment programs appear to be targeted for a relatively young and well-educated population. (Most recent U.S. Census Bureau data lists the median years of school completed for persons 25 years of age and older, and for all races, as 12.5 years; Statistical Abstracts, 1981). While the correlation of effect size with education is small ($r$ = .129, $p$ = .003), it appears that outcome is greater for less educated subjects. A similar trend (r significant but less than .10) favoring young subjects was observed regarding age; the relationship between age and outcome requires further study.

A particularly significant finding concerned subject diagnosis. Enrichment is generally targeted for "normal and healthy" couples and families: To quote Sawin, "enrichment is the process of strengthening marriages and families, of deepening attributes that persons and family systems already possess, to provide further growth of the individual and marital or family system" (p. ii, 1979). Whether enrichment "works" with clinic or distressed populations has yet to be empirically established; hence, this variable was included in the present analysis.

Twenty-five studies reported from 0 to 100% of their subjects were distressed ($\overline{X}$ = 34%). Analysis of variance was run grouping studies into two categories, not distressed to 34%, and 35% and greater. Effect size for the more distressed population was .51, while effect size for the less distressed group was .27. This difference was found to be significant ($F$ = 12.17, $p$ = .001). If this finding is given further support in future research, then the use of enrichment interventions in conjunction with marriage and family clinics deserves serious consideration. The dual caution is also added that not all couples and families are "enrichable" (L'Abate & Weeks, 1976), and while serving a preventive function, enrichment cannot prevent all ills; enrichment claims therefore need to be kept modest (Smith, Shoffner & Scott, 1979).

Additional descriptive characteristics of the enrichment population were noted. Thirty-eight studies reported from 56% to 100% of adult participants were in their first marriage ($\overline{X}$ = 86%). Only one study assessed the effectiveness of a step family enrichment program (Sheehy, 1981). Thirty-four studies reported from 73% to 100% of adult participants indicated some religious preference ($\overline{X}$ = 94%). The target population thus appears to constitute a group with relatively intact marriages having strong identification with religious institutions.

Inadequate numbers of studies prevented examination of the question of what points in the developmental life cycle do enrichment programs show greatest, most lasting effects. In the family life cycle only the family with teenagers warranted particular attention (8 studies).

### Research Design

Meta-analysis provides the researcher with the opportunity to examine the influence of research design and statistical analyses were significantly related to outcome; no differences in outcome were associated with treatment group size, types of assignment or controls, recruitment procedures or dropout rates.

Design rating was based on the Gurman and Kniskern (1978) rating system. The correlation for design rating with outcome ($r$ = .101, $p$ = .002) indicated a small relationship between effect size and better designed studies.

Largest effect sizes were found for studies using simpler forms of statistics, t-tests (ES = .57), while smallest effects were associated with more complex analyses, multivariate analyses (ES = .21). This is understandable as the primary motivation for using such complex analyses is the search for small, yet stable, effect sizes.

Additional observations were noted for recruitment and mortality, two frequent problems for enrichment programming and research. Recruitment was less a problem for those studies offered within or to a specific setting, i.e., school, church, or agency than for programs simply offered to a broader community.

Correlations were run for several variables thought to influence mortality rates. Mortality was found to be positively correlated with adult age, years of marriage, length of program, and program structure. Said differently, dropout rates were greatest for older subjects with more lengthy marriages, participating in some lengthy and structured programs. Mortality was negatively correlated with leader experience level; that is the more experienced leaders tend to have less problems with participants dropping out. Finally, large mortality problems were reported by those researchers using mailing procedures to gather post-test and follow-up data.

## Measurement

When examining factors related to outcome, the most powerful proved to be measurement issues. Significant differences were observed based on participant self-evaluation versus non-participant rating sources, skill areas versus satisfaction and perceptual areas, and low versus high reliability and validity instrument ratings. Further significant differences were observed in effects over time.

Eight-nine different instruments were examined: 76% of effect sizes were self-report ($n = 833$) and the remainder were behavioral measures ($n = 254$). The most significant difference of the meta-analysis was observed in this comparison ($F = 66.528$, $p = .001$). Behavioral measures such as audiotaping or videotaping were associated with an effect size average of .76, and self-report instruments with an effect size average of .35. Participants appear to see less change in themselves following treatment than do those who observe them.

Instruments were rated for reliability and validity, with ratings ranging from 0 to 4. The Pearson Correlation, ($r = -.117$, $p = .001$) indicated that instruments with lower ratings tended to have somewhat greater outcome. This finding suggests that the most important endeavor of future enrichment research will be to catalogue assessment instruments, weeding out those heavily used instruments having poor discrimination, and examining further those newer instruments indicating promise.

Outcome areas were classified as (a) satisfaction, adjustment; (b)

Table 2
Effect Size by Outcome Area

| Area | ES | s | N |
|------|-----|-----|-----|
| Satisfaction | .343 | .460 | 372 |
| Pers skills | .632 | .797 | 294 |
| Personality | .231 | .424 | 110 |
| Other | .490 | .400 | 11 |

Table 3
Effect Size by Outcome Area by Gender or Role

| Outcome Area | Male ES | N | Female ES | N | Parent ES | N | Child ES | N |
|------|-----|-----|-----|-----|-----|-----|-----|-----|
| Satisfaction | .498 | 106 | .329 | 106 | .379 | 15 | .134 | 15 |
| Per skills | .624 | 55 | .607 | 57 | 1.045 | 51 | .822 | 39 |
| Personality | .163 | 74 | .187 | 74 | .382 | 5 | .053 | 11 |
| Other | .373 | 7 | .214 | 7 | .965 | 2 | .370 | 4 |

relationship skills, communication and problem-solving skills; (c) personality variables; and (d) other (Gurman & Kniskern, 1977). We hypothesized that relational skills would be easier to influence than either satisfaction or personality variables. Perhaps relational skills might be considered as antecedents to the latter variables. Effect size was in fact significantly higher for relational skills ($F = 17.43$, $p = .001$). In addition, when outcome area was broken down by gender, men and women scored similarly for personality measures and relationship skills, however, men scored significantly higher than women on satisfaction measures ($t = 2.18$, $p = .05$).

The question of the durability of enrichment-induced change was examined by comparing post-test and follow-up scores. Thirty-four studies (40%) included follow-up measures totalling 276 effect sizes. Table 4 compares post-test (ES $= .44$) and follow-up (ES $= .34$) effect sizes. While this drop was significant ($t = 2.35$, $p = .05$), follow-up scores did not return to pretest averages. This decrease underlines the need for booster, follow-up sessions to help maintain treatment gains, as called for by Mace and others (1981). Further research is needed to assess durability of effects according to specific outcome areas; for example, are there differential effects for skill areas versus satisfaction measures across time.

Two significant variables omitted from the present study require

Table 4
Effect Size for Posttest and Followup

| Time | ES | s | $\underline{N}$ |
|------|------|------|------|
| Posttest | .437 | .623 | 787 |
| Followup | .336 | .593 | 276 |

further examination on future enrichment research. Reactivity of the measurementinstrument (the degree to which the measurement process affects test taker's behavior and, in turn, the results obtained from measurement) likely bears a significant relationship with outcome (Smith, Glass & Miller, 1980). Likewise, the match between program goals and type of measurement instrument can be assumed to be a key variable.

A number of enrichment studies reported a disruption effect, or a "getting worse" phenomenon following completion of the program (Broxton, 1980; Collett, 1979; Glisson, 1979; McIntosh, 1975; Shoffner, 1976). This was variously described as a temporary period of behavioral and/or cognitive disorganization seeming to result from a disorganization of preconceived notions about marriage and communications, as well as an awkwardness in using newly learned skills. Whether couples and families move through a series of stages of learning and skill acquisition, beginning with disorganization and ending with integration, remains to be tested. Most certainly the issue of timing constitutes a key measurement variable for future enrichment research.

## SUMMARY AND CONCLUSIONS

The current study is the most comprehensive, integrative summary of the enrichment literature to date. The results reported in the previous section refer to univariate relationships between a large number of independent variables and the single dependent variable, effect size. The focus of analysis was main effects rather than interactions. Two factors necessitated this focus. First, since the enrichment field is relatively new, conclusive data have yet to be compiled on main effect relationships. A primary value of this study is to guide and establish direction for further testing of main effects and interactions. Second, the problem with meta-analytic techniques which are post hoc procedures is that the possibility for further analyses depends on the nature of the data. Like a fisherman throwing out a net, the meta-analysis researcher cannot control the nature of the catch.

With these cautions in mind, conclusions are drawn (a) for the participant, (b) for the program leader and designer, and (c) for the researcher. *For the participant.* To quote T.S. Eliot,

> Fare forward, travellers! not escaping from the past
> Into different lives, or into any future;
> You are not the same people who left that station
> Or who will arrive at any terminus . . .

>                     (Four Quartets, p 134, 1971)

Enrichment does make a difference in the lives of participants. Changes will likely be largest in the areas of communication skills, such as speaking for self, active listening, using feeling statements and empathetic responses, and making use of constructive problem-solving techniques; changes will likely be smaller in the areas of marital happiness and satisfaction, relationship quality and intimacy, although these may follow later.

Participants may also undergo negative changes initially, experiencing some disruption in marital or family expectations or some awkwardness in using newly learned skills. For example, parents and teens approach an enrichment program with parents relying on authoritarian styles of leadership and placing a high value on family closeness. Based on participation in the program, parents come to value a shared decision-making process and family atmosphere that allows for greater individual autonomy. These shifts involve considerable realignment of parental expectations. Or a couple may approach a communications program believing they are relatively open with each other. Based on participation in the program they observe that they can be considerably more open and responsive to each other.

*For the program leader or designer.* The 1984 Annual Conference of the American Association for Marriage and Family Therapy included an Institute on the topic, "The Coming Switch to Preventive Services: Implications for Marriage and Family Therapists"; leaders David and Vera Mace challenged clinicians to devote some percent of their time to preventive work, "whether they got paid for it or not" (Mace & Mace, 1984). Napier made a similar plea in the Plenary Session of the previous Annual Conference of AAMFT. The present study lends support to the effectiveness of enrichment, preventive efforts. Changes will likely be in the moderate range, as opposed to the larger changes seen in therapy. As an adjunct to clinical work, enrichment interventions offer the advantage of allowing more people to participate at a lower cost, and because several couples or families are offered services together, the professional's time is used more efficiently.

Some clinicians use enrichment programs for both preventive and diagnostic purposes (L'Abate & Weeks, 1976). That is, what is learned about a couple or family in enrichment can lead to a therapy referral or to presenting alternatives to clients' dysfunctional but not entrenched ways of interacting.

Local program designers or facilitators are frequently faced with the dilemma: to offer a simpler, one or two session format and perhaps draw more participants, or offer an extended, multiple session format and involve fewer participants. The present study indicates that little change be expected for the brief format. Greatest changes can be expected for those programs using an experiential, behavioral rehearsal process; little change can be expected for the lecture and discussion process. If programs run 12 hours or longer they will likely show greater change than the briefer formats. Finally, effects of programs will diminish over time, indicating a need to help participants generalize their gains to the home setting, perhaps using some form of follow-up session(s).

*For the researcher.* The most important contribution research may make to the enrichment field at present is to establish a catalogue system of measurement instruments. Instruments might be classified according to the different kinds of information they provide, i.e., subjective or objective data from either an insider or outsider frame of reference (Olson, 1977). Other dimensions to be assessed would include suitability for both distressed and healthy populations, ability to distinguish time frames of recent past versus previous past, ability to measure change in behavioral, cognitive and/or affect dimensions, and ability to measure global versus specific dimensions of change. Such a catalogue would make more available the scattered information on properties of existing instruments, and would include past records of use in the enrichment field.

Many areas of both main effects and interactions have yet to be empirically tested: subject age and education levels; program structure, particularly for unstructured programs; sequencing of programs (weekend followed by weekly sessions); the fit of specific programs for particular developmental stages, and for distressed populations; the match between instrument and program, and instrument reactivity. The reader should examine the manuscript carefully to note the many variables that, contrary to expectation, were not related to outcome.

The researcher is encouraged to use extended time frames for measurement, ideally spanning a minimum of one year. Within that time frame multilevel assessment of behavior, cognitive and affective change is encouraged. Multilevel assessment should also include individual, dyadic and system levels of analysis.

# REFERENCES

Carnes, P. (1981). *Understanding us: Instructor's manual.* Minneapolis: Interpersonal Communication Program.

Cohen, J. (1977). *Statistical power analysis for the behavioral sciences.* New York: Academic Press.

Eliot, T.S. (1971). *The complete poems and plays.* New York: Harcourt, Brace and World.

Giblin, P., Sprenkle, D. & Sheehan, R. (1985). Enrichment outcome research: A meta-analysis of premarital, marital, and family interventions. *Journal of Marital and Family Therapy, 11,* 257–271.

Glass, G. (1976). Primary, secondary and meta-analysis of research. *Education Researcher, 5,* 3–8.

Guerney, B. (1977). *Relationship enhancement.* San Francisco: Jossey-Bass.

Gurman, A. & Kniskern, D. (1977). Enriching research on marital enrichment. *Journal of Marriage and Family Counseling, 3,* 3–9.

Gurman, A. & Kniskern, D. (1978). Research on marital and family therapy: Progress, perspective and prospect. In S. Garfield & A. Bergin (Eds.), *Handbook of psychotherapy and behavior change* (2nd ed.). New York: Wiley.

Hof, L., Epstein, N. & Miller, W. (1980). Integrating attitudinal and behavioral change in marital enrichment. *Family Relations, 29,* 242–248.

Hof, L. & Miller, W. (1981). *Marriage enrichment: Philosophy, process and program.* Bowie, MD: Brady.

L'Abate, L. & Weeks, G. (1976). Testing the limits of enrichment: When enrichment is not enough. *Journal of Family Counseling, 4,* 70–74.

L'Abate, L. (1981). Skill training programs for couples and families. In A. Gurman & D. Kniskern (Eds.), *Handbook of family therapy.* New York: Brunner/Mazel.

Landman, J. & Dawes, R. (1982). Psychotherapy outcome: Smith and Glass' conclusions stand up under scrutiny. *American Psychologist, 37,* 504–516.

Mace, D. (1981). The long trail from information giving to behavior change. *Family Relations, 30,* 599–606.

Mace, D. & Mace, V. (1984). What is the marriage and family enrichment movement and where is it going? Presentation, American Association for Marriage and Family Therapy, San Francisco.

Miller, S., Nunnally, E. & Wackman, D. (1979). *Couple communication I: Talking together.* Minneapolis: Interpersonal Communication Program.

Olson, D. (1977). Insiders and outsiders' views of relationships: Research studies. In G. Levinger & H. Rausch (Eds.), *Close relationships.* Amherst, MA: University of Massachusetts Press.

Olson, D. (1983). How effective is marriage preparation? In D. Mace (Ed.) *Prevention in human services.* Beverly Hills, CA: Sage.

Sawin, M. (1979). *Family enrichment with family clusters.* Valley Forge: Judson Press.

Schumm, W. & Denton, W. (1979). Trends in premarital counseling. *Journal of Marital and Family Therapy, 22,* 23–32.

Smith, M., Glass, G. & Miller, T. (1980). *Benefits of psychotherapy.* Baltimore: Johns Hopkins Press.

Smith, R., Shoffner, S. & Scott, J. (1979). Marriage and family enrichment: A new professional area. *The Family Coordinator, 28,* 87–93.

Strube, M. & Hartmann, D. (1983). Meta-analysis: Techniques, applications and functions. *Journal of Consulting and Clinical Psychology, 51,* 14–27.

Tallmadge, G. (1977). *Ideabook: The joint dissemination review panel.* Washington, D.C.: Department of Health, Education & Welfare.

Wampler, K. (1982). The effectiveness of Minnesota Couple Communication Program: A review of the research. *Journal of Marital and Family Therapy, 8,* 345–355.

# BIBLIOGRAPHY
## Studies Included in the Meta-Analysis

Abrego, P. (1981). An evaluation of the effects of a family life education program on marital and family relationships (Doctoral dissertation, University of Washington).

Avery, A., Ridley, C., Leslie, L., and Millholland, T. (1980). Relationship Enhancement with premarital dyads: A six month followup. *The American Journal of Family Therapy, 8,* 23–30.

Bader, E., Microys, G., Sinclair, C., Willet, E., and Conway, B. (1980). Do marriage preparation programs really work? A Canadian experiment. *Journal of Marital and Family Therapy, 6*, 171–179.

Barber, C. (1979). Marriage enrichment in the Church (Doctoral dissertation, Talbot Theological Seminary).

Beaver, W. (1978). Conjoint and pseudo-disjunctive treatment in communication skills for relationship improvement with married couples (Doctoral dissertation, Marquette University).

Becnel, H. (1977). The effects of a Marriage Encounter program on marital need satisfaction in regard to role identity, focusing, and self-disclosure in intimacy (Doctoral dissertation, Kansas State University).

Bellamy, D. (1979). The short and long term psychological effects of marriage enrichment on marital adjustment and church related behavior (Doctoral dissertation, East Texas State University).

Bigney, R. (1978). Intrapsychic and interpersonal personality and temperament changes in marital dyads resulting from a marriage enrichment program based on rational emotive therapy (Doctoral dissertation, The College of William and Mary).

Bonjean, M. (1976). The effects of participation in Marriage Encounter's continuous dialogue on marital communication (Doctoral dissertation, Northern Illinois University).

Broadbent, D. (1980). Effects of specific analysis and communication training on marital problem solving and positive interactions (Doctoral dissertation, Florida State University).

Brock, G., and Joanning, H. (1980). Structured communication training for married couples: A comparison of the Relationship Enhancement Program and the Minnesota Couple Communication Program. Paper presented at the National Council on Family Relations, Portland, OR.

Brown, R. (1976). Effects of couple communication training on traditional sex stereotypes of husbands and wives (Master's thesis, Appalachian State University).

Broxton, E. (1980). Marital enrichment: Some research and observations on effectiveness (Doctoral dissertation, Brigham Young University).

Bruder, A. (1972). Effects of a marriage enrichment program upon marital communication and adjustment (Doctoral dissertation, Purdue University).

Burns, C. (1972). Effectiveness of the basic encounter group in marriage counseling (Doctoral dissertation, University of Oklahoma).

Campbell, E. (1974). The effects of couple communication training on married couples in the child rearing years: A field experiment (Doctoral dissertation, Arizona State University).

Carlton, K. (1978). An evaluation of the effects of communication skills training on marital interaction (Doctoral dissertation, University of Utah).

Chidester, C. (1975). A comparison of two treatment methods on the marriage relationship (Doctoral dissertation, Brigham Young University).

Collett, C. (1979). A comparison of the effects of marital and family enrichment programs on self concept and conflict resolution ability (Doctoral dissertation, Purdue University).

Collins, J. (1977). Experimental evaluation of a six month conjugal therapy and Relationship Enhancement Program. In B. Guerney (Ed.) *Relationship Enhancement: Skill Training for Therapy, Problem Prevention and Enrichment.* San Francisco: Jossey-Bass.

Coufal, J. (1975). Preventive-therapeutic programs for mothers and adolescent daughters: Skills training versus discussion methods (Doctoral dissertation, Pennsylvania State University).

D'Augelli, A., Deyss, C., Guerney, B., Hershenberg, B., and Sborofsky, S. (1974). Interpersonal skill training for dating couples: An evaluation of an educational mental health service. *Journal of Counseling Psychology, 21*, 385–389.

David, J. (1981). The effects of a structured family enrichment program upon selected dimensions of psychological functioning of intact families (Doctoral dissertation, Florida State University).

Davis, E. (1979). The short and long term psychological effects of two marriage enrichment group program formats (Doctoral dissertation, East Texas State University).

Dillard, C. (1981). Marriage enrichment: A critical assessment of the Couple Communication Program model (Doctoral dissertation, Virginia Technic and State University).

Dillon, J. (1976). Marital communication and its relation to self esteem (Doctoral dissertation, United States International University).

Dode, I. (1979). An evaluation of the Minnesota Couples Communication Program: A structured educational enrichment experience (Doctoral dissertation, Arizona State University).

Dorlac, C. (1981). A comparison of 2 couples' enrichment programs which differ in their structure over time (Doctoral dissertation, University of Missouri).

94        MARRIAGE AND FAMILY ENRICHMENT

Durrant, G. (1971). The effect of the Family Home Evening Program on the self-images of school age children (Doctoral dissertation, Brigham Young University).

Ehrentraut, G. (1975). The effects of pre-marital counseling of juvenile marriages on marital communication and relationship patterns (Doctoral dissertation, United States International University).

Ely, A., Guerney, B., and Stover, L. (1973). Efficacy of the training phase of conjugal therapy *Psychotherapy: Theory, Research and Practice, 10*, 201–207.

Epstein, N. and Jackson, E. (1978). An outcome study of short term communication on training with married couples. *Journal of Consulting and Clinical Psychology, 46*, 207–212.

Farris, D. (1979). Problem solving skills training for marital couples: An evaluation of a weekend training format (Doctoral dissertation, Texas Tech University).

Fennell, D. (1979). The effects of a Choice Awareness Marriage Enrichment Program on participant's marital satisfaction, self concepts, accuracy of perception of spouses, and choosing behaviors (Doctoral dissertation, Purdue University).

Fisher, B. (1976). The application of four properties of systems theory to family education (Doctoral dissertation, Brigham Young University).

Flemming, M. (1976). An evaluation of a structured program designed to teach communication skills and concepts to couples: A field study (Doctoral dissertation, Florida State University).

Garland, D. (1979). The effects of active listening skills training upon interaction behavior, perceptual accuracy, and marital adjustment of couples participating in a marriage enrichment program (Doctoral dissertation, University of Louisville).

Ginsberg, B. (1977). Parent Adolescent Relationship Development. In B. Guerney (Ed.) *Relationship Enhancement: Skill Training Programs for Therapy Problem Prevention and Enrichment.* San Francisco: Jossey-Bass.

Glisson, D. (1976). A comparison of reciprocity counseling and communication training in the treatment of marital discord (Doctoral dissertation, Washington University).

Grando, R. (1972). The Parent Adolescent Relationship Development Program: Relationship among pretraining variables, role performance, and improvement (Doctoral dissertation, Pennsylvania State University).

Harrell, J. and Guerney, B. (1976). Training married couples in conflict negotiation skills. In D. Olson (Ed.) *Treating Relationships.* Lake Mills, Iowa: Graphic Publishing.

Hawley, R. (1979). The Marriage Encounter experience and its effects on self perception, mate perception and marital adjustment (Doctoral dissertation, University of Nebraska).

Heitland, W. (1977). An experimental communication program for premarital/dating couples (Doctoral dissertation, Ball State University).

Hines, G. (1975). Efficacy of communication skills training with married partners where no marital counseling has been sought (Doctoral dissertation, University of South Dakota).

Huber, J. (1976). The effects of dialogue communication upon the interpersonal marital relationship (Doctoral dissertation, California School of Professional Psychology).

Jesse, R. and Guerney, B. (1981). A comparison of gestalt and Relationship Enhancement treatments with married couples. *American Journal of Family Therapy, 9*, 31–41.

Joanning, H. (1982). The long term effects of Couple Communication Program. *Journal of Marital and Family Therapy*, in press.

Larsen, G. (1974). An evaluation of the Minnesota Couple Communication Program's influence on marital communication and self and mate perceptions (Doctoral dissertation, Arizona State University).

Larson, K. (1976). The effects of communication training in small groups upon self disclosure, marital adjustment, and emotional attachment in marriage (Doctoral dissertation, University of Utah).

Markman, H. & Floyd, F. (1980). Possibilities for the prevention of marital discord: A behavioral perspective. *American Journal of Family Therapy, 8*, 29–48.

McIntosh, D. (1975). A comparison of the effects of highly structured, partially structured and nonstructured human relations training for married couples on the dependent variables of communication, marital adjustment, and personal adjustment (Doctoral dissertation, North Texas State University).

Miller, S. (1971). The effects of communication training in small groups upon self-disclosure and openness in engaged couples' systems of interaction: A field experiment (Doctoral dissertation, University of Minnesota).

Millholland, T. & Avery, A. (1982). The effects of Marriage Encounter on self-disclosure, trust, and marital satisfaction. *Journal of Marital and Family Therapy, 8,* 87–89.

Nelson, R. & Friest, W. (1980). Marriage enrichment through Choice Awareness. *Journal of Marital and Family Therapy, 6,* 399–407.

Neuhaus, R. (1976). A study of the effects of a Marriage Encounter experience on the interpersonal interaction of married couples (Doctoral dissertation, Columbia University Teachers College).

O'Connor, R. (1974). Mother child empathy and problem solving skill training: An evaluation of a developmental model. (Doctoral dissertation, University of Minnesota).

Pearson, D. (1978). A marriage enrichment program: Its effects on the intimacy of couples successfully terminated from marriage therapy (Doctoral dissertation, Brigham Young University).

Rappaport, A. (1976). Conjugal Relationship Enhancement Program. In D. Olson (Ed.) *Treating Relationships.* Lake Mills, Iowa: Graphic Publishing.

Roberts, P. (1974). The effects on marital satisfaction of brief training in behavioral exchange negotiation mediated by differentially experienced trainers (Doctoral dissertation, Fuller Theological Seminary).

Robin, A. (1975). Communication training: An approach to problem solving for parents and adolescents (Doctoral dissertation, State University of New York at Stony Brook).

Samko, M. (1976). Self-disclosure and marital communication as a function of participation in a marriage workshop and subsequent use of a communication technique (Doctoral dissertation, California School of Professional Psychology).

Schaffer, M., Schaffer, W., & Gutsch, K. (1981). The effects of the Minnesota Couple Communication Program on marital communication and adjustment. Unpublished manuscript.

Schlein, S. (1971). Training dating couples in empathic and open communication: An experimental evaluation of a potential preventive mental health program (Doctoral dissertation, Pennsylvania State University).

Schwartz, R. (1980). The relationship among communication style, self-esteem and the Couple Communication Program (Doctoral dissertation, Purdue University).

Seymour, T. (1977). Effectiveness of Marriage Encounter couple participation on improving qualitative aspects of marital relationships (Doctoral dissertation).

Sheehy, P. (1981). Family enrichment for step families: An empirical study (Doctoral dissertation, Purdue University).

Shoffner, S. (1976). Use of videotape learning packages: A marital enrichment field experiment (Doctoral dissertation, University of North Carolina at Greensboro).

Smith, R. (1981). An evaluation of the effectiveness of graduated phase modeling in improving communication skills and self perceived relationship quality among dating couples (Doctoral dissertation, Purdue University).

Sprenkle, W. (1980). A comparison of two preventive programs: Couple Communication Program versus family communication with regard to their impact on family dynamics and marital adjustment (Doctoral dissertation, Purdue University).

Strafford, R. (1978). Attitude and behavior change in couples as a function of communication training (Doctoral dissertation, Texas Tech University).

Stanley, S. (1978). Family education to enhance the moral atmosphere of the family and moral development of adolescents. *Journal of Counseling Psychology, 25,* 118–126.

Steller, J. (1979). The effects of couples communication training upon individualized goals, marriage adjustment, self-disclosure, and the use of communication skills by married couples (Doctoral dissertation, University of Minnesota).

Strozier, A. (1981). The effects of a selected marriage enrichment retreat upon relationship change, marital communication, and dyadic adjustment (Doctoral dissertation, Southwestern Baptist Theological Seminary).

Swicegood, M. (1974). An evaluative study of one approach to marriage enrichment (Doctoral dissertation, University of North Carolina at Greensboro).

Taylor, H. (1977). Conducting and evaluating a family enrichment program for improving the quality of communication (Doctoral dissertation, Eastern Baptist Theological Seminary).

Thompson, K. (1978). The effectiveness of couples communication training on interpersonal orientation, couple communication, perceptual congruence, and verbal communication style: A field study (Doctoral dissertation, University of Iowa).

Travis, R. & Travis, P. (1975). The Pairing Enrichment Program: Actualizing the marriage. *The Family Coordinator*, *24*, 161–165.

Urban, D. (1980). The short term effects of a marital enrichment program on couple communication (Doctoral dissertation, Brigham Young University).

Venema, H. (1975). Marriage enrichment: A comparison of the behavior exchange negotiation and communication models (Doctoral dissertation, Fuller Theological Seminary).

Vogelsong, E. (1975). Preventive-therapeutic programs for mothers and adolescent daughters: A followup of Relationship Enhancement versus discussion and booster versus no-booster methods (Doctoral dissertation, Pennsylvania State University).

Wampler, K. (1979). The effect of ego development on the learning and retention of communication skills (Doctoral dissertation, Purdue University).

Warner, M. (1981). Comparison of a religious marriage enrichment program with an established communication training enrichment program (Doctoral dissertation, Purdue University).

Wieman, R. (1973). Conjugal Relationship modification and reciprocal reinforcement: A comparison of treatments for marital discord (Doctoral dissertation, Pennsylvania State University).

Williams, E. (1975). Parent-teenager communications training project (Doctoral dissertation, University of Minnesota).

Witkin, S. (1976). The development and evaluation of a group training program in communications skills for couples (Doctoral dissertation, University of Wisconsin at Madison).

# Leadership Training for Marriage and Family Enrichment

Preston M. Dyer
Genie H. Dyer

**ABSTRACT.** As the marriage and family enrichment movement has matured issues concerning the selection, training, and certification of leaders have become more important. Early leaders were self-trained; but successful continuation of the movement, requires a systematic approach for training and verifying the competence of practitioners. This process is complicated by the diversity in the field. To illustrate current approaches to training this article presents in detail the training and certification model used by the Association of Couples for Marriage Enrichment and in less detail the models used by Couples Communication Program, Understanding Us, Family Clusters, and Relationship Enhancement.

Recently a young minister approached us after a seminar, "I'm impressed with what I hear about marriage enrichment, and I want to be trained to use it with couples in my congregation. But I'm single. Will that make any difference?" he asked.

"We recently attended our first marriage enrichment retreat," began a letter from a couple in their thirties, "and have decided that we want to be certified leaders. My wife is a licensed psychologist, and I am completing my graduate training in social work. Because of our clinical training, can't we be exempted from the basic training requirements?"

A couple nearing retirement age—he is a salesman and she a clerk—telephoned to say, "We've gotten so much from enrichment. We've been in an active support group for the last five years and have been on a retreat every year. We want to become leaders as a way of giving back a part of what we've received. What do we have to do before we can start leading groups?"

These situations illustrate some key questions in the selection, training, and certification of leaders for marriage and family enrichment programs: Can enrichment, particularly marriage enrichment, be led by single people or unmarried co-leaders, or must it be led by a married couple?

Preston M. Dyer, PhD, ACSW, is Professor of Sociology and Social Work at Baylor University, Waco, Texas. Genie H. Dyer, MS, is Assistant to the Dean for Continuing Education at Baylor University, 76703.

*97*

Must leaders have professional competencies before they can be trained for enrichment? What kinds of specific training best equip people for leading enrichment events?

In the first article published on enrichment training almost a decade ago, David and Vera Mace warned:

> The entire question of the leadership of marriage enrichment programs is so new that the subject must be considered experimental, fluid, subject to change and wide open to discussion. (Mace & Mace, 1976, p. 124)

Because hard research data were not yet available, they advised postponing definitive decisions and dogmatic statements about training, and encouraged experimentation with training models.

Although experimentation has occurred, research has not yet matured to the point that we can ignore the Maces' warning. If the field is to continue to grow, we must address the question of how best to develop leadership. Even though the enrichment literature has greatly expanded in the last ten years, little has been written about training. Our purpose in writing this second-generation article is to provoke discussion on the selection, training, and certification of enrichment leadership.

We begin by identifying and discussing some basic issues related to training for enrichment leadership. Our intent is to raise questions and suggest some possible directions. Second, to illustrate current approaches to training, we describe the training models of four national organizations: The Association of Couples for Marriage Enrichment (ACME); Interpersonal Communications Programs, Inc. (ICP); Family Cluster, Inc.; and the Institute for the Development of Emotional and Life Skills (IDEALS). These organizations have extensive experience in training for enrichment programs and provide examples to illustrate the basic issues.

We have gathered data in several ways. Much of it is impressionistic, based on our own experiences in training. We served four years on the ACME Training and Certification Committee and saw its model evolve. We also experienced three of the models firsthand: ACME, ICP, and Family Cluster. Correspondence and personal conversations with Bernard Guerney of IDEALS, David Mace of ACME, and Margaret Sawin of Family Cluster produced additional information, as did descriptive material provided by various training programs.

## KEY ISSUES IN ENRICHMENT TRAINING

Three basic questions are critical to leadership training: Who should be trained for leadership? What should that training consist of? How should competence be determined and recognized after training? These questions are not independent of each other. How one is answered certainly affects the other; however, we discuss them separately below under the general headings of selection, training, and certification.

## Selection

Professional vs. lay leadership, and couple vs. non-couple leadership are the two main issues in selection. The first is important in all forms of enrichment; the second is central to marriage enrichment.

Founders of the movement, although self-trained in enrichment, have been professionals in their own right. Beyond these early leaders, however, selection has not emphasized prior clinical training.

One concern in training people without clinical competencies for enrichment leadership is the potential of harm to participants. Mental health professionals have questioned not only the effectiveness of enrichment but also what dangers it might hold for participants (see Furey, 1983). Although no one has yet produced any strong evidence of serious harm, this threat must be taken seriously and rigorously investigated.

The potential for harm may be less in the marriage encounter model than in more interactive models. Since this model does not permit couples to share their experience in the group, leader couples are responsible only for giving their testimonies and not for the group interaction process. The actual direction of the group is in the hands of professional clergy (who may or may not be clinically trained).

David Mace's decision to train laypersons for his more interactive model was based on his successful experience in training nonprofessionals for the Marriage Guidance Center in Britain during World War II. More recently, Bernard and Louise Guerney and their colleagues have demonstrated the efficacy of using nonprofessionals to teach sophisticated social skills in various applications of relationship enhancement (Guerney, 1982).

A general assumption in the field has been that the development of the enrichment movement has depended primarily on nonprofessionals. This may not be correct. Although professional certification in one of the human services has not generally been a prerequisite for enrichment training, many current leaders have professional credentials. For example, ICP dropped its certification requirement for instructor training in 1981 because they found the knowledge and skill level of those applying for training was such that both Couples Communication and Understanding Us could be taught without attending a training workshop (ICP, 1982, p. 3). Additionally, an informal review of ACME files on certified leaders suggests a similar situation. Out of eighty-one certified couples, in 53% of the cases both spouses have credentials as either a psychologist, social worker, marriage and family therapist, nurse, physician, pastoral counselor, or teacher. In only eleven cases (13%) do neither husband nor wife hold professional certification.

These findings from ICP and ACME, linked with the fact that all marriage encounter programs include a clergyperson, suggest fewer enrichment events are led by nonprofessionals than some in the field have assumed.

The second major issue in the selection process is that of married couples vs. individuals or unmarried co-leaders directing marriage enrichment events. Those who strongly advocate couple leadership cite modeling as a primary advantage. Married couple leaders have the advantage of working on real-life marital concerns in front of participants so that their behaviors and attitudes toward each other demonstrate as much as their words. Also, in programs which depend on group interaction, a couple's willingness to be vulnerable and to open their marriage to the group has the advantage of breaking down reluctance to discuss intimacies with strangers. On the other hand, programs that are primarily lecture or skill development may gain little from married couple leadership.

We are aware of no strong research evidence that documents the benefits of using married couples in enrichment, marital and family therapy, or even sex therapy. However, most studies that have considered the issue have done so from the one therapist vs two therapists standpoint and have used unrelated therapists. The efficacy of married couple to married couple work remains virtually unexplored.

Our experiences in marriage enrichment leads us to favor couple leadership. We agree with a friend who said, "Leading a marriage enrichment experience singly seems almost a contradiction in terms." Beyond the advantages discussed above, we find joint leadership much less demanding than working alone. While one concentrates on one activity the other is free to observe or to consider what needs to be done next. Moreover we find working together using a participatory style enriches our own relationship.

## *Training*

How does the field go about training leaders once it has settled these questions about selection? The diversity among programs makes it hard to answer the questions for the field as a whole. Some programs are highly structured and leaders need only to follow detailed manuals. Others are loosely structured and require leaders skilled in group facilitation. Family enrichment requires skills of working with adults and children simultaneously. Obviously, training needs for these programs differ. Consequently, training in the field is currently program-focused; that is, one learns how to lead a specific program.

As the field develops, a more unified approach to training will be needed. Putting more emphasis on process and less on program will help. A review of the enrichment literature suggests that practitioners have given more attention to the formats of enrichment than to understanding the process by which relationships are enriched (see Hof & Miller, 1981). Much more research into the enrichment process is needed; with better understanding of the process, training models can be based on process, not on program characteristics.

Currently, the favored approach to training is a laboratory-apprenticeship model. Typically, training workshops consist of two parts. First, an experienced trainer(s) leads the trainees through the actual enrichment program for which they are being trained. Second, trainees assume the leader role and practice on their fellow trainees. Family Cluster is an exception to this, since trainees practice on actual families instead of on other trainees.

Generally, training is experiential rather than academic or theoretical, with little emphasis on knowledge of enrichment literature other than that related to a specific model. As a result, leaders often have a narrow view of the field. What may be needed is an approach that combines academic rigor with experiential learning. Eastern Baptist Theological Seminary is experimenting with such a model.

Some leaders in the field have speculated the field may need two types of enrichment leaders: (1) practitioners with primarily experiential training; and (2) scholars (teachers, theoreticians, researchers) and who may also be practitioners. If the enrichment field is to gain the respect of the professional community and of academic disciplines, scholars are surely needed. Individuals with strong academic preparation are essential if we are to be rigorous in testing our assumptions and challenging our affirmations. This does not imply, however, that every person who leads an enrichment event must have that academic training.

## Certification

"I have all the certifications I need," a psychology professor said during a discussion of certification procedures. "Why should I go through all of this?" This comment illustrates what may be the chief issue for certification: whether to certify at all. The woman making this comment had met the requirements necessary for recognition by her own professional association and by the licensing board of her state. Of what value to her is certification in enrichment?

Certainly, certification is not legally required to lead enrichment. Anyone who chooses can organize and lead an event. Currently, certification, like training, is offered by organizations which sponsor specific programs. For example, ICP provides certification for leaders of the Couples Communication and Understanding Us programs; and ACME certifies couples to lead marriage enrichment events. These organizations provide certification to assure particpants that programs will be delivered as designed and tested, by competent leaders. The benefit to the individual leader depends on the national prominence of the organization and the value its name has in association with his/her enrichment work. Additionally, organizations refer clients to certified leaders.

Certification may have more meaning for people without professional sanctions. "Until we were trained and received certification, I really did not feel like a full partner with my husband," said the wife of an experienced family social worker. "Going through the training and certification process gave me confidence I needed." As this statement indicates, certification can mean more than just the satisfactory completion of the training process.

A second issue in certification is how to determine competence. The officials of some programs do not want to certify because they do not believe they have the means to evaluate competence. Lacking that ability, they do not want to be in the position of attesting to competence by certification. These organizations simply provide a certification of training.

Organizations which do certify require satisfactory completion of training plus evidence of successful performance in leading events. In the following discussion of training and certification models, we will see this done in two ways: (1) through the traditional supervisory model; and (2) through evaluation by participants in events led by the trainee(s).

## LEADERSHIP TRAINING MODELS

In this section, we discuss the four training models mentioned earlier. Because of our familiarity with the ACME model, it is presented in more detail than the others. We hope this highly developed and structured model will provide a basis for continued discussion beyond this article. The other three models, although presented in less detail, provide a source for comparison.

### ACME Leadership Training Model

ACME trains and certifies leader couples (not individuals) for marriage enrichment. Its Training and Certification Committee (T & C Committee)—composed of four to six couples appointed by the Board of

Directors to serve rotating terms—sets standards and acts on applications for certification.

In its standards document,[1] ACME identifies the type of marriage enrichment events for which it provides training (ACME, 1982, p. 1);

1. The event should be led by one or more qualified married couples, reflecting an interacting, participatory leadership style.
2. The method should be basically experiential and dynamic, rather than didactic and intellectual.
3. There should be occasion for couple interaction within the context of the group and private couple dialogue.
4. Structured experiential exercises may be used either to initiate dialogue or in response to it.
5. There should be one leader couple for each four to eight participant couples.
6. Participant couples should have some voice in determining the agenda.
7. Planned session time should cover at least 15 hours.

## Selection

ACME looks for the following qualities in selecting leader couples (ACME, 1982, p. 1 & 2):

1. . . . committed to marital growth and are currently working effectively on their own marriage.
2. . . . function well as a team, cooperating smoothly and not competing or getting in each other's way.
3. . . . communicate a warm and caring attitude to other couples in the group.
4. . . . ready to share their own experiences, to be open and make themselves vulnerable if necessary.
5. . . . sensitive to group members and group process.
6. . . . have some basic knowledge of human development, marital interaction, and group process.

A leader couple and two trainer couples evaluate trainees prior to full certification. Some of ACME's basic assumptions are evident in these criteria. The couple's ability to work effectively and cooperatively is a major concern. One partner may be highly skilled and quite capable of handling any situation occurring in a group; however, if he/she cannot function with the partner as a cooperating team, they cannot meet selection requirements. Further, couples who are participatory in their leadership style and willing to make themselves vulnerable are considered to be better leaders.

## Leadership Training

The ACME training model was patterned after the Marriage Communication Lab (MCL) training model developed by Antoinette and Leon Smith (Smith, 1976). The Smiths used their model to train Methodist ministers and their wives to promote MCL in Methodist churches and asked David and Vera Mace, founders of ACME, to work with them. Later the Maces and Smiths helped develop the ACME training model while serving on the T & C Committee.

Training takes place in two residential workshops—Basic and Advanced—which must meet prescribed standards (ACME, 1982, p. 2). The Basic Training Workshop prepares trainee couples to lead a particular marriage enrichment model. Generally, the model is presented in the form of the weekend retreat, because that event is considered to be the most intensive and difficult format to lead.

In the Basic Training Workshop, five to eight couples work with a certified basic trainer couple in an intensive forty-hour laboratory training experience. First, the couples share a fifteen-hour enrichment experience led by the trainers, followed by six hours of learning basic concepts, group dynamics, methods, and techniques. In the next nine hours, each couple designs a program and leads a group composed of fellow trainees. Finally, each couple engages in a "marital exploration dialogue." In this one to one-and-a-half-hour, in-depth dialogue, the two discuss with each other their potential for leadership and areas of vulnerability and growth in their relationship. This takes place in an atmosphere of trust and openness in the presence of two to four other trainee couples and at least one member of the training team.

Following the Basic Training workshop, trainees are considered leaders in training. They must wait one year and lead at least two events meeting the previously mentioned standards before attending an Advanced Training Workshop. The purpose of Advanced Training is to move the couple beyond the single model experience of the Basic Workshop to an understanding of the entire marriage enrichment process. This thirty-hour workshop provides trainees the opportunity to: (1) reflect on their leadership experiences, (2) identify their strengths and needed growth areas, and (3) increase their knowledge and skills in the enrichment process. Less structured than the Basic Workshop it focuses on the particular needs of the trainees involved. This includes exploring current research, literature, and theories of the field to enhance their own leadership styles. Emphasizing the process underlying enrichment, the trainees are encouraged to explore different models and vehicles for using that process. To accomplish this, advanced trainers must be experienced and knowledgeable in a variety of enrichment models.

## Certification

ACME certifies couples at five levels: provisional and full certification, basic trainer, advanced trainer, and trainer supervisor. Couples are eligible for provisional certification after they have attended one event as participants and satisfactorily completed the Basic Training Workshop. This certification requires a positive evaluation from the leader couple of the event and from the trainers. The evaluation is based on a numerical ranking of husband and wife on the following eight items (ACME, 1980b):

1. Contributes positively to a healthy growing marriage relationship.
2. Contributes to cooperative teamwork with partner.
3. Comes across as a warm and caring person.
4. Effectively communicates understanding and insights to others.
5. Ready to be open in sharing marital experiences.
6. Sensitive to needs of other couples in the group.
7. Copes effectively with a difficult situation.
8. Demonstrates effective planning and design skills.

Full Certification is based on a positive evaluation from the trainer couple for the Advanced Training Workshop and positive evaluations from participants in five marriage enrichment events led by the trainee couple. The trainers for the Advanced Training Workshop evaluate the couple on the above criteria plus six others (ACME, 1980a):

1. Has realistic knowledge about themselves as a couple.
2. Shows evidence of learning from previous leadership experiences.
3. Shows evidence of marital growth and identification of areas in marriage to be strengthened.
4. Is familiar with marriage enrichment models and shares resources.
5. Is familiar with and can articulate marriage enrichment theory and practice.
6. Is familiar with group theory.

The trainee couple's ability to function as enrichment leaders is evaluated by the consumers of their services. Trainee couples provide ACME with a list of all couples who participate in their events. These participants are asked by mail to evaluate the couple. The evaluation consists of narrative comments and a Likert-type ranking of the following items (ACME, 1980c):

1. What was your overall impression of the leader couple?
2. How did the leader couple cooperate together as a team?
3. Did the leader couple come across as warm and caring?
4. How sensitive were the leaders to the needs and concerns of the group?
5. Was the leader couple open in sharing their marriage?
6. How well did the leader couple organize the program and use the time?
7. Did the leader couple give you a confident feeling that they would be able to handle a difficult situation in the group?
8. Would you recommend couples who were friends of yours to enroll in a marriage enrichment event with this leader couple?
9. Are you fully agreed as a couple about the way you have checked the replies?

In making decisions on certification, members of the Training and Certification Committee use the following: evaluations of a leader couple, evaluations of basic and advanced trainer couples, a summary of evaluations of couples who have participated in events led by the applicants, the couple's self-report on continuing education (books read, seminars attended, etc.), and the couple's initial application for training and certification. In most cases, this documentation provides relatively clear evidence of the couple's ability or inability to meet selection standards and to function as leaders. Once certified, leaders must reapply every three years. Recertification requires documentation of continuing enrichment and education activities and a self-evaluation of leadership.

In the last two years, ACME has developed certification standards for basic and advanced trainer couples. Previously, the founders of the organization did this. As the need expanded, they chose co-leaders to assist them in training; and eventually the co-leaders became accepted trainers. It became evident, however, as still more people sought training, that standardization of this process would be necessary. In July 1984, the Committee approved selection, training, and certification procedures for basic and advanced trainers and for trainer supervisors. The latter are couples approved to supervise basic and advanced trainer internships.

To be certified as a basic or advanced trainer, a couple must complete internships under a certified trainer supervisor. Fully certified leaders who have successfully led a minimum of four events in the past three years may apply for a basic trainer internship. To be certified at this level, the couple must complete two internships and develop an acceptable design for a Basic Training Workshop. An internship basically means leading a workshop with a trainer supervisor. To be eligible for an advanced trainer internship, the applicant couple must have demonstrated creativity in the development and/or leadership of a variety of models and forms of marriage enrichment; must have been certified basic trainers for two years; and must have successfully led a minimum of four basic training workshops in the last two to five years. One internship is required for the advanced trainer. Selection and certification of trainer supervisors is based on a high level of performance as a trainer, documented by positive evaluations from participants in workshops.

Certification at any level may be suspended or withdrawn when evidence is submitted that a couple is not providing effective leadership for marriage enrichment events. Standards require couples be given a full explanation of the reasons for such action. Any action taken by the T & C Committee may be appealed to the ACME Board of Directors.

## Other Training and Certification Models

Relationship Enhancement and the Couples Communication Program are frequently discussed as marriage and family enrichment programs. To us they are only tangentially related to marriage and family enrichment, since targeted participants are not necessarily married couples or families. However, both programs develop important social skills with documented effectiveness. Relationship Enhancement is used in therapy, in enrichment with families and couples, in training foster parents, and in other applications where social skills are important. The Couples Communication Program has been adapted for teaching interpersonal communications in almost any situation. Social skills development, particularly communication skills, is an essential part of marriage and family enrichment—but not all of it. We present these programs, however, because many do see them as marriage and family enrichment progams and because they provide additional approaches to training and certification.

## Couples Communication and Understanding Us

Interpersonal Communications Programs, Inc., (ICP)[2] developed and promotes the Couples Communication Program (Miller, Nunnally, & Wackman, 1979) and Understanding Us (Carnes, 1981), a family enrichment program. Both are highly structured. Instructors have a manual setting out a step-by-step agenda, complete with timing. Instructions for exercises are explicit, and detailed text material is provided. ICP provides training workshops through approved training associates, but this is no longer a requirement for certification.

To become ICP certified, an instructor (an individual or couple) must instruct four groups. Three of these groups are considered intern groups and the trainee submits only self-evaluation forms. These are reviewed by ICP staff, who give feedback to the trainee. In the last session of the fourth group, participants anonymously evaluate the instructor on ICP forms, which the instructor collects and returns to ICP. The certification decision is based on the instructor's self-evaluation and the evaluations of the participants.

## Family Clusters

Family Clusters is a family enrichment program developed by Margaret Sawin (Sawin, 1979). The program is unique in bringing together (clustering) four or five complete family units. Clusters meet together over an extended period of time for educational experiences related to living in family type relationships. It is a powerful program for contemporary families. It includes any family life style—single, reconstituted families, etc.—and provides intergenerational experiences.

Family Clustering, Inc.,[3] provides training for this family enrichment program. Two training formats are available. Preferred is a week-long laboratory held in a residential setting. The laboratory provides trainees with experience as members and leaders of a cluster.

The alternative training experience is a 30-hour Family Cluster Training Workshop. This format includes four or five basic "skill shops" for learning skills and theory related to family clusters. Included as well are two demonstration sessions with families who join the workshop for an afternoon and evening. Training in both formats includes: family systems, practice in skills to lead family groups, designing for experiential learning, and intergenerational group dynamics.

Family Clustering, Inc., does not have a certification program. Once the individual has experienced the training, he/she is free to begin developing and leading family clusters.

## Relationship Enhancement

Bernard Guerney, Jr., who developed Relationship Enhancement (RE), describes it as follows:

. . . . systematic instruction in a set of skills designed to achieve personal and group goals, to improve personal and interpersonal adjustment, and to help participants to help others do the same. (Guerney, 1982, p. 483)

Training and certification in RE is available through the Institute for the Development of Emotional and Life Skills (IDEALS).[4] Training takes place in a three-day, beginning workshop and a two-day, advanced workshop. Professionals, paraprofessionals, and laypersons are accepted. Training includes explanation, demonstration, modeling, supervised practice, and homework. Once trainees integrate the skills into everyday living, they are supervised by a trainer in the process of passing the skills along to others. After successfully completing the advanced workshop, trainees receive 24 to 36 hours of supervision either through co-leadership, live observations, or audio tapes. Certification is based on the trainee's satisfactory completion of supervision. RE is closer to traditional professional training models than the other models discussed because of its "hands-on" supervision.

## CONCLUSION

We have reviewed four approaches to training and certification for enrichment programs. These four programs are at varying stages of development. Family Clustering provides training but no certification. Interpersonal Communications, Inc., provides certification for its two programs but does not require specific training. IDEALS and ACME require two training sessions. IDEALS requires up to 36 hours of direct supervision, whereas ICP and ACME determine competence by the evaluations of consumers. All four programs use a laboratory approach to training. Certification attests only to meeting the standards of a specific organization. No legal restrictions exist on who can or cannot lead marriage and family enrichment.

These four programs illustrate not only different approaches to training but also the diversity of programs in the enrichment field. This diversity accounts for much of the difficulty in resolving the issues discussed in the first section. This diversity has been good for expanding the field, but has resulted in a program-oriented approach to training. If the field is to continue to mature, it needs a more unified approach to leadership development. For this to occur, process must be emphasized and formats de-emphasized. It is probably still too early to disregard the Maces' warning against moving too quickly toward a restrictive approach to leadership training; however, it is high time for the various enrichment groups to begin dialogue on the issues. We personally share Luciano L'Abate's hope for the future (1983, p. 62):

. . . that eventually we may succeed in producing new identities whose main personal and professional objectives will be to prevent rather than to "cure" and whose calling will be as honored, respected, and valued as any other healing profession.

## FOOTNOTE

1. Copies of this document can be obtained by writing to ACME, P.O. Box 10596, Winston-Salem, N.C. 27108.
2. Interpersonal Communications, Inc., 1925 Nicollet Ave., Minneapolis, MN 55403.
3. Copies of this document can be obtained by writing to ACME, P.O. Box 10596, Winston-Salem, N.C. 27108.
4. Interpersonal Communications, Inc., 1925 Nicollet Ave., Minneapolis, MN 55403.
5. Copies of this document can be obtained by writing to ACME, P.O. Box 10596, Winston-Salem, N.C. 27108.
6. Interpersonal Communications, Inc., 1925 Nicollet Ave., Minneapolis, MN 55403.Copies of this document can be obtained by writing to ACME, P.O. Box 10596, Winston-Salem, N.C. 27108.
7. Interpersonal Communications, Inc., 1925 Nicollet Ave., Minneapolis, MN 55403.
8. Copies of this document can be obtained by writing to ACME, P.O. Box 10596, Winston-Salem, N.C. 27108.
9. Interpersonal Communications, Inc., 1925 Nicollet Ave., Minneapolis, MN 55403.
10. Family Clustering, Inc., P.O. Box 18074, Rochester, N.Y. 14618-0074.
11. IDEALS, 2630-C Clyde Ave., State College, PA 16801.

## REFERENCES

ACME. (1980a). *Advanced trainers' evaluation form.*
ACME. (1980b). *Basic trainers' evaluation form.*
ACME. (1980c). *Questionnaire to couples who have participated in a marriage enrichment event.* Winston-Salem, NC: Author.
ACME. (1982). *Standards for the training of marriage leader couples for marriage enrichment retreats and growth groups.* Winston-Salem, NC: Author.
Carnes, P. J. (1981). *Understanding us.* Minneapolis: Interpersonal Communication Programs, Inc.
Doherty, W., & Lester, M. E. (1983). Researchers support casualty claim. *Family Therapy News, 14*, 8.
Furey, R. J. (1983). Reevaluating marriage encounter: Can claim of casualties be validated? *Family Therapy News, 14*, 8.
Guerney B. (1982). Relationship enhancement. In E. K. Marshall and P. D. Kurt (Eds.), *Interpersonal helping skills* (pp. 483–492). San Francisco: Jossey-Bass.
Hof, L., & Miller, W. R. (1981). *Marriage enrichment: Philosophy, process, and program.* Bowie, MD: Robert J. Brady Co.
ICP Staff. (1982, March). Participation in CC/UU instructor workshop no longer required. *Relationship Education*, p. 3.
L'Abate, L. (1983). Prevention as a profession: Toward a new conceptual frame of reference. In D. R. Mace (Ed.), *Prevention in family services: Approaches to family wellness* (pp. 49–62). Beverly Hills: Sage.
Mace, D. R., & Mace, V. (1976). The selection, training, and certification of facilitators for marriage enrichment programs. *The Family Coordinator, 2*, 117–125.
Miller, S., Nunnally, E. W., & Wackman, D. B. (1979). *Talking together.* Minneapolis: Interpersonal Communication Programs.
Sawin, M. (1979). *Family enrichment with family clusters.* Valley Forge: Judson.
Smith, L., & Smith, A. (1976). Developing a national marriage communication lab training program. In H. A. Otto (Ed.), *Marriage and family enrichment: New perspectives and programs* (pp. 241–253). Nashville: Abingdon.

# Marriage Enrichment:
# Rationale and Resources

### Sandra Diskin

**ABSTRACT.** Marriage enrichment programs have developed as a response to a multitude of technological, religious and social shifts in our society. They exist and attract participants with the goal of enabling basically good marriages to expand and grow. Within the body of this article, historical background is offered to explain the need for these services. Descriptions of several models are given and discussed with pertinent references and resources for the practitioner interested in incorporating a program into his or her practice.

## INTRODUCTION

Within the framework of the family is reflected the rapid change that characterizes our modern society. The marriage enrichment movement helps couples respond to these changes. Enrichment programs teach partners interpersonal skills and build empathetic respect between individuals within the marital relationship. Spouses are then able to create a supportive environment for each other allowing them to respond more fully, both as an individual and as a team, to the challenges confronting them.

Historical background is offered in this article as a description of how changes in basic patterns of society have affected marriages. Enrichment models are presented reflecting the diversity of interest and focus within the movement itself and programs are discussed along with a list of resources available to the practitioner.

In the interest of brevity, the focus of this article is upon *marriage enrichment* alone and excludes many fine programs in *family enrichment*. Family life education programs have also been excluded for the same reason and because such programs are usually oriented toward information-giving rather than development as are marriage enrichment programs. As Mace observed (1981), it is a " . . . long, long trail from information-giving to behavioral change" (p. 599).

---

Sandra Diskin, PhD, is Director of Counseling of Family Associates, Box 2386, West Lafayette, IN 47906.

## MARRIAGE IN TRANSITION

The ways in which marriage partners relate to each other have changed significantly with the advent of industrialization and technological advancements. Work shared by couples during the agricultural revolution became separated during the industrial revolution. The value of home centered skills, traditionally women's work, lessened as wage earners could buy needed products and services from providers outside the family. Also, the foundation of the family has been threatened, Lasch (1977) asserts, by withdrawing the functions of childbearing, education and counseling from family members and relegating these to societal institutions. As interdependence and function diminished, emphasis was shifted to love and nurturance as the basis of establishing and maintaining a family (Ogburn, 1933).

Similarly, the industrial age changed family patterns as the extended family did not have the mobility and adaptability necessary for the industrial age (Toffler, 1980). Consequently, the "modern" model in all industrial societies became what has become known as the nuclear family—father, mother, and a few children with no encumbering relatives.

The result of industrialization upon the family, then, is twofold. First, greater burdens were placed upon the marital relationship as social supports were attenuated or lost. Second, the "glue" of functional integration ceased to exist. That is, marriage was reduced to one essential function, that of providing love and nurturance to the partners.

While change does not imply crisis, it does mean difference. And differences have surfaced with the change in traditional family roles and all of the attendant alterations in relationships brought about by these changing roles. Marriage has evolved in recent times through three stages (Mower, 1977)—from arranged marriages, through marriage based on love and, finally, to the "companionship" marriage. The reality of the arranged marriage was functional integration. Romantic marriage implied a static relationship and the ideal of " . . . and they lived happily ever after," a "fit" of spousal personalities. The companionship marriage, however, brings the implication of *two* people putting effort into the relationship to achieve individual and couple growth.

## CREATING NEW MODELS

As the institution of marriage changed, so have the skills necessary to function effectively within the marital relationship. Traditional marriages based upon functional and integrated work roles of the spouses have given way to expectations of companionship between partners. Previous behavior patterns need to be augmented or replaced through new learning in order to live successfully within this new model. Moreover, intimacy is often pursued as a new "ideal" within modern marriages (Schafer and Olsen, 1981). Good marital communication and the ability to solve problems in a sharing way were two skills which were not as vital to earlier generations, yet they are basic for today's intimate relationships.

The traditional marriage with rigidly defined roles was simple, because the rules of the "institution" were clearly defined by society. Berger (1963) explains, "Institutions serve as a regulatory agency, channeling human actions much in the same way instincts channel animal behavior. Institutions provide procedures through which human conduct is patterned, compelled to go . . . " (p. 87). Not only was the "institution" defined, but role function within the confines of that institution was defined. Mace (1979) describes the old pattern by indicating, "Avoidance of conflict was . . . reinforced by defining gender roles so as to keep the sphere of husband and wife, father and mother, separated to avoid disagreement" (p. 410).

People faced with these certainties could either choose the pattern or choose against it. The most difficult choice is to initiate a new form which involves second order change (Watzlawick et al., 1974). A radical departure from established patterns invalidates an existing system and creates a new one which, once set in motion, cannot be recalled. Within the old system, marital problems were peripheral to the need for stability. Marital problems today challenge the stability of the institution, and the fragility of today's marriages attests to changed expectations.

## THE SEARCH FOR MARITAL GROWTH

The economic and procreative alliance that once characterized marriage has now largely given way to the idea that partners can share their lives in an intimate way. Marriages once held together by forces outside the relationship are now expected to be sustained and nourished by resources within the relationship. The issue is no longer stability, but growth and potential within the partner dyad.

Marital enrichment programs make this new goal possible—they make companionship marriages workable (Mace, 1975). These programs encourage couples to create their own relationships within boundaries meaningful to them. Rather than imposing standards of behavior from the outside, they draw marital goals from the couple that are internally consistent and congruent with each person's value system and behavioral possibilities.

The popularity of these programs and the enthusiasm of participants testify to the need for information, skills building, and intimacy enhancement which the programs provide. The marital enrichment "movement" is especially timely in that old established patterns of relating are crumbling but few meaningful models exist for guiding contemporary couples to build new patterns. Widespread public interest in discovering different models is reflected in the fact that books such as *Open Marriage* (1972) by the O'Neills have become best sellers.

## A LEARNING ENVIRONMENT

Since marriage enrichment programs provide skills and models for partners in their search for a new kind of relationship, different types of programs have evolved. At the core of all of them, however, is an opportunity for couples to experiment with new ways of relating. Participants are encouraged to expand their possibilities with each other in a supportive environment. To this end, most successful programs use leaders both as participants and as models for the skills they propose to teach (Hof and Miller, 1980). Enrichment programs usually adhere to an educational model, teaching skills of communication, conflict negotiation and decision making. They act as a support service for marrieds, enabling partners to better cope with increasing demands placed upon them both from within and without the relationship.

Traditionally, professionals have provided these programs as an adjunct to counseling services. The major difference is that enrichment is aimed at the functional marriage as a preventive measure, rather than at the dysfunctional marriage as a remedy. Marriage enrichment is for those who want to get deeper into a marriage relationship, not out of it!

## A PLETHORA OF PROGRAMS

The movement to "make good marriages better" (Dale and Dale, 1978) has expanded rapidly in a few short years. Reflecting their diverse philosophical or religious origins, various techniques are utilized that range from silence and contemplation, to problem solving and play therapy. Couples are taught skills and encouraged to use these while building on positive feelings in the relationship. Most are based on an assumption that couples, while not dysfunctional, often interact at less than fully satisfying levels. Marriage enrichment seeks to enhance devitalized marital relationships and treat them in a preventative manner before they need rescue.

It is difficult to generalize about the current marital enrichment programs in existence. Some are highly structured, some change with the experience of the leader or composition of the couples' group. There are group sessions with couple interaction, and some designed so that the partners will only encounter each other. There are even leaderless group experiences intended to be guided by readings or cassette tapes made for this purpose.

Program variations also stem from the orientation of the presenter. Enrichment experiences usually spring either from religious groups or university sponsored programs. There are weekend retreats, semester classes, and short courses. Some focus on communication, others on repressed anger, still others on the joy within the marital relationship. Two things seem to hold constant and these are: the search for the possible relationship, and the delight of exploring new paths together.

Following are some brief descriptions of programs, organizations, and resources within the field of marital enrichment.

## COLLEGE PROGRAMS

Most marriage enrichment programs developed through universities are more theoretically based and outcome researched. These are two deficits of most religiously oriented enrichment experiences. An evident shortcoming in most university programs, however, is that they lack a delivery system with the result that they remain local in character. Developed and researched with care, they often spring to national attention with the publication of their program and findings and just as quickly fade from prominence and memory.

### Couple Communication

Happily there are some exceptions to the above generalization. One outstanding example of a college course that is now a widely accepted enrichment experience is Couple Communication (CC), formerly the Minnesota Couples Communication Program. As the title suggests, this learning experience focuses exclusively on couple communications. It targets skills rather than issues. These skills are (1) those which enable partners to understand their rules and interaction patterns (awareness skills), and (2) those which enable them to change their rules and interaction patterns (communication skills).

Although the format may be altered, the usual course meets once a week for sessions lasting three hours. A screening interview for prospective participants is held prior to the first session. Leadership is restricted to certified instructors trained for this purpose. Groups are usually limited to 5–7 couples to allow ample time for group feedback to individual couples practicing their newly acquired skills.

A supportive environment is established early and leaders model the skills to be learned. Couples work in the group setting and are expected to do exercises between sessions and to read passages in the textbook, *Talking Together* (Miller et al., 1979). There is also an instructor's manual available from the same source which is: Interpersonal Communications Programs, Inc., Couple Communication, 300 Clifton Avenue, Minneapolis, Minnesota 55403.

### Relationship Enhancement

Humanistic psychology can be seen as a precursor to many marriage enrichment programs. Central to the philosophy of the human potential movement is the idea that people can express themselves fully and joyously as they grow toward the expression of their potential. Within the growth process is reverence and respect for others who are also striving to reach their personal potential.

The enrichment experience of the Relationship Enhancement (RE) program expands and builds upon these humanistic psychology concepts. An empathic climate is established enabling participants to freely express their feelings. This leads to increased self-acceptance and knowledge which, in turn, leads to increased self-acceptance of others. The approach is aimed at training people to take care of themselves and educating them in additional modes of behaving.

Participants in RE programs are taught to respond with understanding and acceptance in both the speaker and listener roles, to recognize their own feelings and motivations, and to express themselves congruently. Complete acceptance is stressed with respect for the negative as well as positive feelings and is modeled by the leader.

The Relationship Enhancement program can accommodate a wide variety of formats, from weekend marathon sessions to weekly hour meetings. It was developed by Bernard Guerney, Jr. who is Professor of Human Development and Head of the Individual and Family Consultation Center of the Pennsylvania State University. His affiliation is cited here so that inquiries may be directed to him. The program, methods of conducting sessions and evaluation information are all contained in his book, *Relationship Enhancement* (Guerney, 1977).

### Choice Awareness

One program with a new direction has been developed by Richard Nelson of Purdue University. The premise underlying his program is that the quality of relationships is related to the choices we make. Participants are made aware of options within the choices they make and are facilitated to make better choices. Positive results using his materials in a marriage enrichment experience are reported in the *Journal of Marital and Family Therapy* (Nelson and Friest, 1982).

Written material in the program package includes a book explaining Choice Awareness, a workshop guidebook for participants, and a manual of workshop sessions for leaders. Audio cassettes are also included in the kit and introduce each of the 16 sessions presenting the key ideas.

*Choice Awareness Workshops* are offered with a 30 day return privilege on all materials from: Guidelines, 545 Wise Road, Schaumburg, Illinois 60193.

### Creative Marriage Enrichment

The Creative Marriage Enrichment Program was developed by Larry and Millie Hof. The program has been tested and used at the Marriage Counsel of Philadelphia, among other places. It is a multi-approach strategy using a Rogerian emphasis in working with couples in a group process that incorporates behavioral techniques. Drawing upon Schutz (1966), issues of inclusion, control, and affection are the core around which they develop their strategies. A complete description of the program including a schedule, exercises, handouts and evaluation procedures are found in their book, *Marriage Enrichment: Philosophy, Process and Program* (Hof and Miller, 1981).

### Other Programs

Marriage enrichment workshops have been offered at universities for purposes of providing research into marital interaction. Although based upon precedents within the field of marriage and family therapy, most of these have never been formalized courses of study for enrichment groups. One such program entitled, "Marriage Enrichment Workshop: A Behavioral Approach," was reported by Dixon and Sciara (1977) with appropriate outcome research. As the title implies, this 8 week course (2 hours weekly) focused upon behaviorally prescribed interactions including communications exercises, identification of mutually satisfying experiences, and negotiating reciprocity exchanges.

Another approach is that of Adam and Gringras (1982) who devised an enrichment program resting upon a theoretical model which targets both the individual contract of the spouses (expectations of the other) and the interactional contract of the couple (modes of relating). The aim of the 8 week, 2-1/2 hour sessions was to enhance awareness, to strengthen communication and to teach negotiation and problem solving to partners.

One program that found its way into much of the literature is Mardilab, short for Marriage Diagnostic Laboratory. Based upon Rogerian principles it uses literature, questionnaires, role-plays, communication exercises, movies, and brief lectures with discussion periods. Participants submit anonymous question cards which direct much of the session time. Couples meet weekly for 5 weeks (2 hour sessions). A description of the program, its resources and foci are contained in an article by Stein (1975).

A program that is unique in that it is intended to enrich the sexual relationship of partners as well as other aspects of their life together is the Pairing Enrichment Program (PEP). Its format was designed to fit into two different time frames, either a weekend retreat, or 3-hour sessions twice a week. PEP is an eclectic approach to marital health and purports to draw from the authors' own experiences in marital and sexual research. An outline of their sessions is contained in the article by Travis and Travis (1975).

### Purist Programs

The many perspectives of differing theoretical stances are to be observed in marital enrichment programs designed around their basic tenets. For example, a behavioral exchange program was reported by Harrel and Guerney (1976). Participants were taught how to identify issues and negotiate a behavioral exchange. A "learning package" was developed for this program which contains readings, instructions for skill-furthering exercises, as well as self/partner forms for evaluating the home skill practice sessions.

A report on transactional analysis used with a marital enrichment group is given by Capers (1976). Possible resources for this type of group are forwarded by Berne (1964) with structured exercises contained in a book by James and Jogeward (1973).

The Gestalt perspective was used in a marriage enrichment program (Zinker and Leon, 1976), that was different from most in that it dealt with many negatives in the marital relationship. The originators facilitated couples in expressing chronic repressed anger and then taught them conflict management skills. The exercises they used are contained in the body of their article.

Systems Marriage Enrichment requires not only leadership training in the contents of the program, but also in the underlying systems concept. This is a flexible program of goals with suggested techniques. A report and description of this alternative model to marriage enrichment is given by Elliott and Sanders (1982).

## RELIGIOUSLY ORIENTED PROGRAMS

The impact of churches outside of their traditional religious concerns has, perhaps, been greater in the marriage enrichment movement than in any other area. The retreat model that many enrichment experiences use as a format is one employed by religious institutions for a long time.

From one standpoint, the church gave birth to marriage enrichment. Father Calvo of Spain and David Mace, working with the Quakers, both led the first marriage enrichment retreats in 1962. When Father Calvo's Marriage Encounter, as it was called, was transplated to this country in 1967, it spread rapidly. As synagogues, and churches of other denominations, became acquainted with Marriage Encounter, they adapted and adopted it so that we now have Jewish Marriage Encounter, Episcopal Marriage Encounter, etc.

### Marriage Encounter

Marriage Encounter weekends are highly structured and, although presented in a group setting, each partner "encounters" only the other in private. There is minimal opportunity for discussion with other participants. The format consists of a series of written husband-wife dialogues preceded by 10–14 mini-lectures by a priest (or other clergy) and husband-wife leader couple. Trust and acceptance is stressed through opening one's self to one's spouse in the written projects. The end result for most couples is the development of an intense atmosphere of intimacy and a renewed sense of commitment to each other.

Marriage Encounter assumes the primacy of the family in human life and the overwhelming significance of the marital relationship. Love is taught to be an action rather than a feeling—an active reaching out to the other. It also celebrates marriage as central to God's plan and a connection to a larger purpose. As the weekend progresses, participants are led from encounter with self, to encounter with partner, to encounter with God, to encounter with world.

For further information and/or a schedule of programs, write:

National Marriage Encounter
955 Lake Drive
St. Paul, Minnesota 55120

World Wide Marriage Encounter
3711 Long Beach Boulevard
Long Beach, California 90807

Christian Marriage Encounter
1913 E. 17th Street
Santa Ana, California 92701

Jewish Marriage Encounter
199 Boston Avenue
Massapequa, New York 11758

## Marriage Communication Labs

The basic design of this program is the retreat model which accommodates ten couples and two leaders. Marriage Communication Labs (MCL) use guided discussion, communication skill building, role-plays and group-process as well as awareness and sensitivity training. A sacred dimension is also stressed within the marital relationship and most MCLs conclude with an informal worship service. Content and methods vary with the lab, depending upon the concerns of the particpants and the skills of the leaders.

Two aspects of the program that distinguish it from other programs are: first, they facilitate partners into talking about sex by showing a film about communication and sexuality. Second, they teach communication in conflict resolution.

A packet of materials containing exercise sheets and outlines for mini-lectures is available. Further information can be obtained by writing: United Methodist Church, Marriage Communication Labs, Board of Discipleship, P.O. Box 840, Nashville, Tennessee 37202.

## The Quaker Format

This marriage enrichment experience has a minimum of structure and no advance planning. Participants are free to shape the entire program to their own needs. Leaders, however, are trained and conduct the retreats much in the same manner from session to session across the country.

Participants are taught to speak from the "I" position and learn not to analyze, judge, confront, or give advice to their partners. Primary interaction is between husband and wife, although they are with each other within a group setting. Sharing within the group is voluntary and feedback may be solicited or declined as each person desires.

Negotiation skills are modeled by the leader couple (husband and wife) with an emphasis on the positive. Mutual affirmation is an important aspect of this program. Closeness within the context of this model is expressed as mutual understanding rather than "togetherness."

Founders of the Association of Couples for Marriage Enrichment (ACME) are David and Vera Mace who developed this marriage enrichment program, commonly called the ACME model. ACME's address is listed in the following section on National Programs.

## Other Programs

Although not originating as a church outreach, the More Joy in Your Marriage Program has traditionally been offered through church auspices. This marriage enrichment experience utilizes trained leaders using group methods to actualize human potential targeted at the marital relationship. The marriage, as shared by the participants, is conceptualized as often bogged down in routines, habits and daily pressures. Otto (1976), who developed this program, believes that through better communication and understanding couples can be helped to make their relationship a source of joy.

The program is described in the source just cited. Other resource books are Otto's *Group Methods to Actualize Human Potential* and *More Joy in Marriage*. For materials and leadership packet to accompany the book write: The Holistic Press, 8909 Olympic Boulevard, Beverly Hills, California 90211.

Another church oriented program is Marriage Renewal Retreats (Schmitt and Schmitt, 1976). An assumption of this approach is that as couples experience themselves in the workshop, their relationship is healed. The act of participation, in and of itself, is one that brings a couple closer. They have changed the name from Marriage Enrichment Retreats to Marriage Renewal Retreats with the belief that one weekend can make the difference.

The visual model they present to participants is one depicting a dynamic relationship pattern. They propose that spouses cycle through affirmation of self to connection with the other as marriages mature. They teach that each excursion into self-discovery allows a deeper and renewed commitment to the other.

For reprints of the article describing the model (about 25¢) ask for: *Conflict and Ecstasy: A Model for a Maturing Marriage*. The address is: Abraham A. Schmidt, 165 S. Fourth Street, Souderton, Pennsylvania 18964.

Finally, the Franciscan Community offers many cassettes, films, books and booklets which are useful in marriage enrichment programs though they do not have a formally developed program of marriage enrichment as such. They are, obviously, Roman Catholic in content and are the work of Clayton Barbeau. *Creating Family* is the name of his film series and also the title of a set of 16 booklets. His many cassette series include titles such as, "Intimacy, Identity and Awareness," "You and I—Here and Now," "The Marital Commitment" and "The Flow of Feelings." For a complete list of materials, please write: Franciscan Communications, 1229 South Santee Street, Los Angeles, California 90015.

## NATIONAL ORGANIZATIONS

Several national associations have been formed to promote marital enrichment. Rather than espouse a particular technique these parent organizations promote the idea of strengthening marriages through working with others who uphold this ideal.

## Association of Couples for Marriage Enrichment

Perhaps the oldest and best known of this group is ACME, the Association of Couples for Marriage Enrichment, founded in 1973 by David and Vera Mace. A non-profit, non-sectarian organization, it has members throughout the United States, Canada and several other countries. ACME invites membership from any couple, individual or organization with a concern for better marriages to join them and share in their programs and resources.

The purposes of ACME, as stated in their brochure, is to enable couples to unite in common interest to: (1) support and help each other in seeking growth and enrichment in their own marriages, (2) promote and support effective community services to foster successful marriages and (3) improve public acceptance and understanding of marriage as a relationship capable of nurturing personal growth and mutual fulfillment. These goals, as well as the ideals which produced the program, are found in the only book about ACME, *We Can Have Better Marriages If We Want Them* (Mace and Mace, 1974).

Ten other books that are informational as well as self-guided enrichment experiences are offered through the association. Three examples of titles are: *Close Companions—The Marriage Enrichment Handbook, Love and Anger in Marriage*, and *How to Have a Happy Marriage*. Audio cassette tapes are also a part of the resource material that is offered. Each tape is $5.00 and covers enrichment topics as well as workshops for clergy couples.

For more information or membership forms, write: ACME, 459 South Church Street, P. O. Box 1059, Winston-Salem, North Carolina 27108.

A network of organizations offering marriage enrichment programs has been established as CAMEO, Council for Affiliated Marriage Enrichment Organizations. This group is concerned primarily with developing leadership and training standards within the marriage enrichment field. They issue a newsletter and meet annually. The address is the same as for ACME.

## Family Service Organization

Although not formed for the purpose of marital enrichment, Family Service Organization offers nationally recognized programs such as Couples Communication (CC) and Parent Effectiveness Training (PET) through its Family Service Agencies in many communities. They also publish materials in packet form for use in family life education, which is not strictly an enrichment program, but which does offer skills training in some aspects of family life. These modules are intended for use with an ongoing time-limited, multi-session group focused on some family concern. Each Family Service Agency does not offer all programs, but the packets which include outlines, handouts and exercises are available from the national organization which is listed below.

They also have a number of original plays which they take out into the community. The subject matter, centering around family interaction, serves as a stimulus for discussions following the program. This specific outreach program relies upon volunteers for actors, with agency trained volunteers working as facilitators for the discussion. The address is: Family Service America, 44 E. 23rd Street, New York, New York 10010.

## Logos Center and Research Institute

One national support organization acting as a resource center for Christian churches and ministries as well as for mental health centers and family life educators is Logos Research Institute, Inc. A non-profit organization and self-described as a "think-tank," their activities range from facilitating grant applications for researchers to teaching classes and distributing information that enhances effectiveness within human relationships and family life. Although listing their offerings under the title of Family Life Education, the emphasis is congruent with the concept of marriage enrichment. Logos Center states in its brochure, " . . . much of the demand for crisis counseling can be averted by investing time in systematic programming focused on prevention and the development of family strengths."

To this end, they offer resources of books, booklets, surveys for self-assessment, audio tapes and a newsletter. They list ten books which range from $2.95 to $6.95 and include such titles as *How to Treat Your Family As Well as Your Friends* and *How Do You Say I Love You.* Especially interesting for enrichment groups might be the *Building Family Strengths* series written around six characteristics of strong families drawn from the research of Dr. Stinnett (1979). Simply written, the materials can be easily understood by people of all educational levels.

Their address is: Logos Research Institute, P.O. Box D, 210 Southwind Place, Manhattan, Kansas 66502.

## The National Jewish Family Center

The National Jewish Family Center conducts research, training and public education programs for Jewish families and counselors. They publish a newsletter and issue publications on issues central to Jewish family life.

For additional information contact: William Petschek, National Jewish

Family Center, The American Jewish Committee, Institute of Human Relations, 165 East 56th Street, New York, New York 10022.

## Other Organizations

A small group entitled Family Enrichment Bureau (a non-profit, interfaith organization) is just beginning with a newsletter, *Learning and Growing Together*, and offers both recorded and printed materials for in-the-home and church use. Free reprints are available to pastors for sampling.

One package of recorded programs they offer come five to the set and is entitled, *Our Marriage Is You and Me*, which charts stages in marital relationships. The tapes are intended as a starting point and an organizer for marital dialogue. They come with directions for use. This particular set sells for $41.25. The address is: Family Enrichment Bureau, Inc., 1615 Ludington Street, Escanaba, Michigan 49829, Phone (906) 786-7002.

The national YMCA has reorganized their Family Communications Skills Center putting it under the Director of Program Services. Their new offering is Positive Partners and can be accessed by writing: John Ferrell, YMCA of USA, 101 N. Wacker Drive, Chicago, Illinois 60606.

## CONCLUSION

As seen from the listings within this article, many programs have developed with the goal of enriching marriages. No one yet knows the full potentialities for growth in couple relationships. But the enthusiasm of couples involved in marriage enrichment suggests that the search for a deeper, more intimate relationship is worthwhile and fulfilling.

## REFERENCES

Adam, D., and Gringas, M. (1982). Short and long term effects of a marital enrichment program upon couple functioning. *Journal of Sex and Marital Therapy, 8*(2), 97.

Berger, P. (1963). *Invitation to sociology: A humanistic perspective*. Garden City, New York: Doubleday and Company, Inc.

Berne, E. (1964). *Principles of group treatment*. New York: Grove Press.

Burgess, E., and Locke, H. (1945). *The family: From institution to companionship*. New York: American Book Company.

Capers, H., and Capers, B. (1976). Transactional analysis tools for use in marriage enrichment. In H. Otto (Ed.), *Marriage and family enrichment: New perspectives and programs*. Nashville: Abbingdon Press.

Dale, R. and Dale, C. (1978). *Making good marriages better*. Nashville: Broadman Press.

Dixon, D., and Sciara, A. (1977). Effectiveness of group reciprocity counseling with married couples. *Journal of Marriage and Family Counseling, 3*(3): 77–84.

Elliott, S., and Sanders, B. (1982). The systems marriage enrichment program. An alternative model based on systems theory. Family Relations, *31*(1): 53–60.

Guerney, B. (1977). *Relationship enhancement*. San Francisco: Jossey Bass.

Harrel, J., and Guerney, B. (1976). Training married couples in conflict negotiation. In D. Olsen (Ed.), *Treating relationships*. Lake Mills, Iowa: Graphic Publishing Company.

Hof, L., and Miller, W. (1981). *Marriage enrichment: Philosophy, process and program*. Bowie, Maryland: Brady Company.

James, M., and Jongeward, D. (1973). *Winning with people, group exercises in transactional analysis*. Reading, Massachusetts: Addison-Wesley Publishing Company.

Lasche, C. (1977). *Haven in a heartless world*. New York: Basic Books.

Mace, D. (1981). The long long trail from information-giving to behavioral change. *Family Relations, 30*, 4.

Mace, D. (1979). Marriage and family enrichment: A new field? *The Family Coordinator, 28*, 409–419.

Mace, D., and Mace, V. (1976). Marriage enrichment: A preventative group approach for couples. In D. Olsen (Ed.), *Treating relationships*. Lake Mills, Iowa: Graphic Publishing Company.

Mace, D. (1975). Marriage enrichment concepts for research. *The Family Coordinator. 24*, 171–175.

Mace, D., and Mace, V. (1974). *We can have better marriages if we want them*. Nashville: Abingdon Press.

Melville, K. (1983). *Marriage and family today* (3rd ed.), New York: Random House.

Miller, S., Nunnally, E., and Wackman, D. (1979). *Talking Together*. Minneapolis: Interpersonal Communications Programs.

Mower, E. (1977). The family: Its organization and disorganization. Quoted in Lasch, C. *Haven in a heartless world*. New York: Basic Books.

Nelson, R., and Friest, W. (1982). Marriage enrichment through choice awareness. *Journal of Marital and Family Therapy, 8*, 87–89.

Ogburn, W. (1933). The family and its functions. *Recent social trends in the United States*, Report of the President's Research Committee on Social Trends. New York, p. 661.

Ogburn, W. (1964). *On culture and social change*. Chicago: University of Chicago Press.

O'Neill, N., and O'Neill, G. (1972). *Open Marriage*. New York: Evans.

Schaefer, M., and Olsen, D. (1981). Assessing intimacy: The pair inventory. *Journal of Marital and Family Therapy, 7*(1), 47.

Schmitt, A., and Schmitt, D. (1981). Marriage renewal retreats. In H. Otto (Ed.), *Marriage and family enrichment: New perspectives and programs*. Nashville: Abingdon Press.

Schutz, W. (1966). *FIRO (the interpersonal underworld)*. Palo Alto: Science and Behavior.

Smith, R., Shoffner, S., and Scott, J. (1981). Marriage and family enrichment: New professional area. *The Family Coordinator, 7*(1), 47–60.

Stein, E. (1975). Mardilab: An experiment in marriage enrichment. *The Family Coordinator, 24*, 167–170.

Stinnett, N. (1979). In search of strong families. In N. Stinett, B. Chesser and J. DeFrain (Eds.), *Building family strengths*. Lincoln: University of Nebraska Press.

Travis, R., and Travis, R. (1975). The pairing enrichment program: Actualizing the marriage. *The Family Coordinator, 24*, 2.

Toffler, A. (1980). *The third wave*. New York: Wm. Morrow and Company, Inc.

Watzlawick, P., Weakland, J., and Fisch, R. (1974). *Change*. New York: W. W. Norton and Company.

Zinker, J., and Leon, J. (1976). The gestalt perspective: A marriage enrichment program. In H. Otto (Ed.), *Marriage and family enrichment: New perspectives and programs*. Nashville: Abingdon Press.